❋ HANDBAGS ❋

Roseann Ettinger

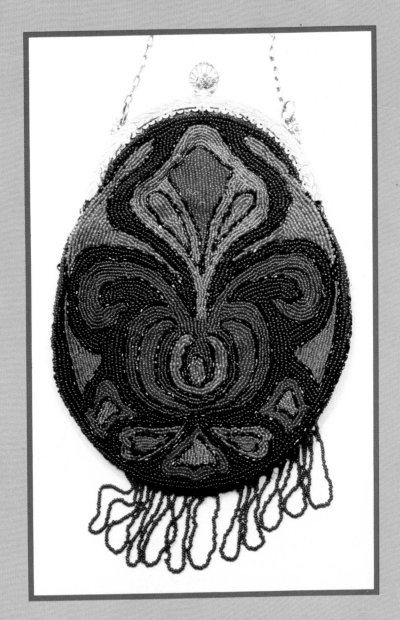

1469 Morstein Road, West Chester, Pennsylvania 19380

Dedication

To My Beloved Grandmother,
Rosanna Rickey,
For the initial inspiration.

Pink glass beaded bag with embossed
floral designs on nickel silver frame.

Title page photo:
Egg-shaped bag fashioned with bright-
colored Bohemian glass beads on net
background, nickel silver frame and
chain handle.

Copyright © 1991 by Roseann Ettinger
Library of Congress Catalog Number: 91-65659.

Printed in the United States of America.
ISBN: 0-88740-372-7

Published by Schiffer Publishing, Ltd.
1469 Morstein Road
West Chester, Pennsylvania 19380
Please write for a free catalog.
This book may be purchased from the publisher.
Please include $2.00 postage.
Try your bookstore first.

We are interested in hearing from authors
with book ideas on related subjects.

Acknowledgments

I would like to take this opportunity to thank my parents, Vito and Marie Rodino, for their encouragement and support during this project. A million thanks to my wonderful children, Clint and Amber Lee Ettinger, for their understanding and patience, and to my husband, Terry Ettinger, for being the understanding man that he is.

My sincere appreciation to the following people who graciously allowed me to photograph some wonderful examples found throughout this book: Amber Lee Ettinger; Christine Ketchel; Peg Harnack; John Morse Jr.; Marceline Lotman and George Wurtzel (Her Own Place).

Special thanks to all the wonderful people at The Big Picture Company, Mt. Laurel, New Jersey.

Back strap pouch made of black velvet with raised silk and metallic embroidery, snap closure and satin lining.

❧ Preface

Three miniature gatetop framed bags made of beadlite enamel, ring mesh and beaded crochet. *Amber Lee Ettinger.*

Many books have been written over the years on the evolution of fashion. There are few books, however, that deal exclusively with accessories that were necessary to complete a fashionable look. *Handbags* was written to survey the evolution of the handbag with its utilitarian and decorative features being appreciated by men and women centuries ago.

The sequence begins with the appended bags and pouches worn by crusaders and nobles in the Dark Ages. Early bags, chatelaines and pockets were worn by women throughout the Middle Ages. Hand carried reticules became popular in the late eighteenth and early nineteenth centuries. The beginnings of the modern handbag, as we know it today, are evidenced in the second half of the nineteenth century. Further division is included which specifically deals with collectible beaded, mesh, leather, needlepoint, tapestry and early plastic handbags.

Collecting handbags has become increasingly popular throughout the last decade. Showing the desire to learn more about them, collectors have required information. Many handbags were hand-made but a large majority were manufactured for the masses. A tremendous amount of manufacturers were responsible for producing handbags in the early twentieth century. This volume chronicles some of the most popular manufacturers and is intended to sharpen the eye and spark curiosity.

Values

To place a value on a handbag or purse, one must consider a multitude of factors. The material with which a particular accessory is made is of prime importance. Hand-made versus machine-made technique, country of origin, stature of the manufacturer, and identifying marks leading to the date of manufacture are also considered. The rarity and complexity of design is taken into consideration as well as the overall condition of the piece. If a handbag previously belonged to someone famous, this factor is also important in estimating the value. Collecting handbags has become a serious hobby in the last few years.

Prices also vary dramatically from one locale to another. Therefore, a value guide, rather than a specific price guide, will be included in the back of the book.

✤ Contents

Mini finger ring purse made of German silver.

Chapter I:

❧ Handbags up to the Twentieth Century

The evolution of handbags, as we know them today, began centuries ago. As early as the Middle Ages, purses were carried by men as well as women. Not always referred to as a handbag, the purse, bag, pouch, almoner, pocket, pocketbook and reticule were some of the early terms used to describe a receptacle that men and women utilized to carry their small personal belongings.

In medieval times the items carried rarely included money; only a select few were lucky enough to possess this commodity. Men used appended bags and pouches of leather to carry important papers and documents. Women carried work or utility bags to house their lace and sewing implements. Other bags and pouches were designed specifically for holding medicines, sachets, snuff, tobacco, fans and keys. Special bags were even constructed for holding relics and prayer books (called reliquary bags) and very personal bags were designed for holding hair combings. These early bags were made of leather, fur and cloth ornately garnished with tassels, bells, fringe and exquisite embroidery. Gold and silver threads created sumptuous metallic embroidery on these utilitarian appendages. Careful scrutiny reveals that fragments of pre-existing ecclesiastical vestments or wall hangings from Western Europe were sometimes transformed into these early bags and pouches, while others were newly made for their specific purposes.

The bags constructed for men were generally larger and some even more elaborate than those made for women. Different social standings and class distinctions sometimes accounted for the elaborateness of this early accessory. Some bags and pouches were attached to rigid ornamental metal frames made of gold, silver, bronze, steel and iron and often inscribed with devotional sentiments. Frequently, chains were attached to the bag with a hook to the belt or girdle, making them more secure, less likely to be stolen.

The medieval practice of giving *alms*, defined as "something given freely to relieve the poor", paved the way for a receptacle known as the alms-bag or almoner. Originally, an almoner was a high-ranking official responsible for distributing money, food or clothing. Later, the bag he carried took on the name which has also been spelled *almonier*, *aumônière* or *amônière*.

The almoner bag was used predominantly by Crusaders and nobles intermittently throughout the Middle Ages encompassing the Gothic period and the Renaissance. Specifically designated as a bag for carrying gold coins, the almoner was given by members of the clergy to Crusaders who distributed the coins to those in need. The bag was constructed of silk, linen, velvet or a host of leathers and suspended from belts or girdles by heavy cords or chains. Medieval embroidery in various forms including chain, stem, satin, split, herringbone and knot stitches enriched these early purses. They became so elaborate that a pictorial survey of the times could be observed through interpretation of the forms depicted on them. One French example of an alms purse dating from the early Renaissance garishly depicts a monster playing a

Handwoven floral tapestry bag with intricate sterling silver frame, English hallmarks, with ring tab closure and link chain. The inside of the bag houses a second frame which is attached to the main hinge mechanism separating the inside of the bag.

Opposite page:

Red velvet pouch-type bag with base metal frame and chain handle, marked M W G in script lettering. This bag is rather new but made very similar to earlier examples.

Medieval alms-bag, 14th century. (Drawing by Maureen Bell).

Floral handkerchief bag made in the shape of a pocket decorated with Bisque doll. 20th century.

tambourine, a bearded man and a half woman/half bird. These figures symbolized the sins of "Avarice, Vanity and Frivolity." Other almoners of the same period were decorated with figures embroidered in gold and silk; characters taken from medieval poetry depicting romantic chivalry of the period. Later, it became fashionable for ladies of affluence to carry almoners containing food or money and to aid those in dire straits.

Use of appended bags and pouches was common throughout the Middle Ages. Pouches were usually small and flat and attached close to the waist, while a somewhat larger bag or sack was suspended from the waist by long cords, sometimes hanging well below the knee. Around the fifteenth century, the European city of Caen, located in northwestern France, was held in high esteem for its magnificent embroidered bags and pouches. Because of their sumptuous nature, Caen-made bags had become the talk of all Europe. Highly acclaimed was a woman known as "Margaret the emblazoner" who was mentioned in early French inventories for her superb skills in executing handmade pouches decorated with coats of arms. Sometimes called *tasques*, they were made of luxurious velvets in splendid colors and garnished with gold and silver threads. They were sold to the nobility and the wealthy aristocrats. By the sixteenth century, the demand for bags and purses grew; guilds were established all over Europe solely devoted to making purses and bags.

During this period, bags termed "pockets" were fashioned for women. Literary works mention *poket, pucket, placket, poke* and *palke* when referring to appendages for women made of cloth such as linen, cotton, canvas and flannel. Pockets made of white dimity and calico prints were mentioned in early colonial inventories. Pear-shaped pockets with rounded corners and triangular-shaped pockets with squared corners were common.

Pockets were usually constructed in pairs attached by ties or tapes to the undergarment and worn concealed under the skirt and petticoat. A vertical slit in each side of the skirt gave access into the pockets which had a corresponding vertical slit. Because these pockets were concealed, they were usually not elaborate. Their functional quality intrigued the women who were competing with men for the number of pockets that men's garments had. It had been said that "Men carried with them thirteen pockets!"

Certain occasions prompted women and young girls alike to display their hand work skills on pockets with embroidery. For many centuries, different embroidery techniques were utilized. The beginner sometimes used simple crewel-work (which became fashionable in New England in the eighteenth century), while the more able embroiderer used a host of other stitches creating complex patterns. Many early pockets were signed and dated by the proud maker. To stumble upon a find such as this would indeed be a compliment to anyone's collection today.

Alice Morse Earle, in her book *Costume of Colonial Times*, however, disagreed that pockets were concealed when she wrote that "pockets were ornamental bags, which were fastened on the outside of the gown." These pockets were decorated with cross stitch on canvas and beads and bugle work on velvet. Obviously, the more elaborate examples were just too pretty to be worn concealed.

Elaborate embroidery was a very fashionable hobby of Elizabethan women in England in the sixteenth century, yet embroidery also was practiced by men in "royal court settings as well as for domestic use." Professional craft guilds were extremely common in medieval Europe.

In the seventeenth century, an interesting type of embroidery surfaced, which was believed to have been started in Italy. Called "stump work", it was made with patterns padded with horsehair or wool forming unique designs in high relief. Made in the Stuart tradition, stump work was found on bags

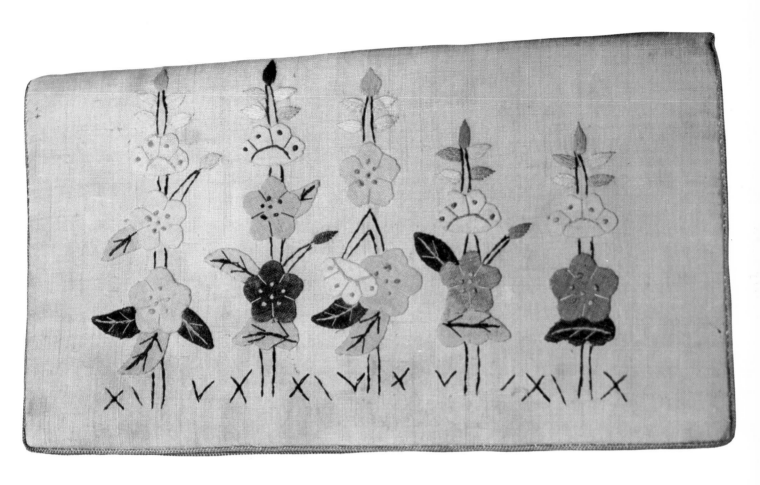

and pouches in addition to decorative pieces such as mirrors, trinket boxes and trays. Biblical and mythological scenes were often garishly depicted as well as flora and fauna. By the second half of the eighteenth century, stump work was a lost art form.

As fashions evolved over the centuries, men's garments began to be designed with numerous pockets so that bags, pouches and even almoners became somewhat disregarded. By the early seventeenth century, pockets sewn into men's greatcoats and puffed breeches served similar purposes and were ultimately more convenient.

Women's pockets were made large and women tended to overload them with some of the oddest things. Numerous items such as mirrors, fans, comforters, smelling salts and liquor flasks were among the items that New England women kept in their pockets. In the late eighteenth century, pockets were such important features of feminine attire that they were mentioned in wills and bequeathed to friends and relatives. These pockets were not designed to hold money. When the need arose for a receptacle for coin or currency, a special purse developed called the pocketbook. This was a flat, rectangular clutch-type bag resembling an envelope with a flap. Basically, it was an early wallet. Used by both men and women, pocketbooks were occasionally enriched with embroidery or made of various leathers. A leather pocketbook advertised in the 1780s made of red Morocco leather contained an "Etwees" (etui), an ornamental case used for holding scissors, knives, toothpicks, tweezers and earpicks. Gradually, numerous items, besides money, were housed in pocketbooks which were then stuffed into the already-bulging pockets.

Linen envelope-style pocketbook decorated with applique and four embroidery stitches.

Embroidered burlap pouch, drawstring is missing.

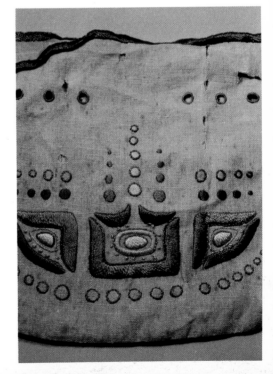

"LOVE'S YOUNG DREAM."

Close up view of Victorian handbag made of beige and black silk with double top handles, front of bag worked with ribbon fashioned with intricate floral arrangements.

Empire fashion; woman holding drawstring reticule, circa 1810.

With the constant overloading of women's pockets and pocketbooks, the female shape became distended. Fashion wise, something needed to be done to alleviate this distressing problem. By the end of the eighteenth century, fashions changed so that voluminous skirts gave way to a narrow silhouette. There was definitely no room for bulging pockets on these new garments. So a new bag, designed to be worn on the outside of the skirt, came into vogue.

In 1804, a London journal commented on these new bags:

> "While men wear their hands in their pockets so grand, the ladies have pockets to wear in their hand."

What this little rhyme made reference to was the *reticule*. Reticules, also called "indispensibles" because they became universally popular in a brief period of time (and then termed 'ridicules' by the French for obvious satirical reasons), were bags gathered at the top with drawstring handles. They were made of many materials such as horsehair, spun steel, satin, velvet and a thin but durable silk known as *sarcenet*. Reticules were elaborately garnished with different forms of embroidery as well as beads, bullion, spangles and sequins known at that time as *pailettes*. Many of the textile varieties were homemade, but with the growing demand for this new accessory, manufactured leather varieties were often preferred; shops selling dry goods began to specialize in leather reticules as early as the 1820s.

Reticules became essential articles of feminine attire during the First Empire in France, the neoclassical period from 1804 until 1814 under the rule of Napoleon I. Thin, sheer and gauzy high-waisted fashions, made popular during the reign of Empress Josephine, became the newest mode. These diaphanous gowns of muslin, poplin and bombazine were so thin and sheer that pockets were, indeed, out of the question. Instead, the reticule came into vogue. Many unusual shapes began to appear as popularity increased. Some shapes were inspired by classical antiquity and some by the shape of what they were designed to hold. For example, circular-shaped reticules were specifically made to hold the circular fans common in the 1820s, while triangular-shaped reticules were fashionable in the 1830s. Josephine, who was extremely fashion conscious, was said to carry a reticule at all times, thus adding impetus for this new accessory. In her reticule was a handkerchief she always held up to her mouth when speaking or smiling because she was self-conscious about her unattractive teeth.

In 1810, *The Morning Herald* commented:

> "Though it is not the mode for ladies to wear pockets in public...no gentleman would refuse to take hold of the lady's ridicule while she is dancing."

By then, reticules were an indispensable accessory in Europe and it did not take long before American women followed suit. Sporadically during the nineteenth century, reticules were suspended from chatelaine hooks attached to a belt or girdle; more often in the second half of the nineteenth century, however, they were hand carried. Thus the term *handbag* came into use to differentiate an accessory that was hand carried from one that was worn.

For an extremely fashionable look, early reticules were made with the same material as the garment. As early as 1807, a French fashion journal commented that "Indispensibles are still much worn and of the same colour as the dress." Preferred fabrics were silks and velvets with cord handles and tassels or long ribbon drawstrings laced through small rings. The creative woman at home could demonstrate her hand work skills by constructing reticules made with hand-painted satins and embroidered silks. Bead embroidery was beginning to become fashionable and reticules completely encrusted with beads were quite common at this time. Ribbons, fringe, lace, tassels and braids also embellished them. Leather reticules, as mentioned earlier, were in vogue in the 1820s and 1830s while reticules displaying piping were common from 1830 until 1850. Berlin wool work was practiced for many decades in the nineteenth century but was particularly fashionable between 1840 and 1870, so reticules displaying bright colored wool embroidery were modish at this time. Around 1850, dark blue and black velvet reticules were enriched with hand painting or embroidered with metallic threads, gilt or steel beads. By the 1860s and 1870s, reticules embellished with braid embroidery and applique were quite prominent.

In 1856, through the synthesis of quinine, Sir William Henry Perkin, an 18 year old English chemist, stumbled upon a synthetic dye known as aniline purple or mauve. Further laboratory experiments with other substances led to more aniline dyes which were used increasingly to tint fabrics and embroidery threads. By 1858, aniline and other synthetic dyes superceded the natural dyes which had been used for centuries.

In addition to reticules made in the drawstring style, framed ones also became popular between 1820 and 1830. Unusual-shaped bags sometimes

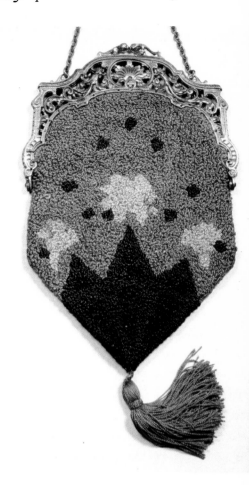

Handbag fashioned with French Knots attached to ornate ormolu openwork frame, marked M R S Co.

Handbag made of black silk and ornate sterling silver frame with cherub designs, marked H & C.

Small Victorian coin purse made of ivory with hand carved ivory rose positioned in center, nickel plated frame, short wooden handle, silk lining, gusseted sides with four inside compartments, marked MS HL.

required the extra support of a metal frame. Pinchbeck, steel, gilt, sterling silver and solid gold frames were employed as well as ivory, amber and tortoiseshell. Some of these frames were further enriched with real or paste gemstones, delicate enamel work, seed pearls and filigree ornamentation. The chain that was attached to the bag was much longer and heavier than the chains found on bags made decades later; sometimes chains were doubled and often the links were very ornate. Dating an early framed reticule requires studying the design, composition, construction and/or decoration. Moreover, hallmarks can be found on early frames, even stamped right into the design of the frame itself. Hallmarks are not just limited to the inside of the frame so careful scrutiny is essential. Personalized or sentimental inscriptions can appear on early metal frames.

As fashion quickly evolved throughout the nineteenth century, confusion with respect to the current accessories sometimes occurred. For example, in the early decades, reticules were essential with Empire style fashions. By the 1830s, however, waistlines dropped to a natural level and skirts were again full with placket holes concealing pockets beneath. This eliminated the need for the reticule for a brief period of time. Individuality still prevailed, however, and women who chose to be unique still carried reticules despite popular demand. By the 1840s, pockets were sewn directly into skirts and this practice, no doubt, was a direct result of the invention of the sewing machine. Also in this decade, small watch pockets were sewn into the waistbands of wide skirts to hold a lady's small pocket watch.

During the following decade, reticules remained somewhat out of fashion as pockets were still used and chatelaine bags were worn suspended from the waist. In 1857, "Railway Safety Pockets" were advertised as being conducive when traveling. Reminiscent of earlier pockets, this detachable appendage was tied around the waist and concealed under the skirt. This was also the period when carpet bags were common among travelers and they were available in wools brightly colored with the new aniline dyes. The development of the railway systems on both sides of the Atlantic Ocean made travel increasingly easy. Bags of all kinds were important to travelers for personal items not packed away in large trunks.

By the 1860s and 1870s, crinolines and full skirts gradually became passe' as bustles appeared, and they allowed no room for side bulges. Reticules again became fashionable. By the 1880s, Alexandra, daughter of the King of Denmark, later consort to Edward VII of Great Britain, and a predominant fashion trend setter, popularized the use of chatelaines. Evolving from the medieval ornament, chatelaine bags created quite an impact on fashion in the fourth quarter of the nineteenth century; (more on this in Chapter II).

Many upper middle class women of the previous century who were able to purchase lavish accessories still chose to use their God-given talents and leisure time creating accessories at home. When they wanted a new reticule, women and young girls alike would spend countless hours labouring on these trivialities. Knitting, crocheting, embroidery and beadwork became favorite pastimes. By the 1890s, a popular novelty in fancy work was lace painting. Upon Spanish, Valenciennes, Nottingham and Fedora laces stunning effects were created by painting and many decorative items and personal accessories were made. Reticules were made to be given as gifts to friends and relatives for special occasions. These little bags were even constructed for men, since the knitted or crocheted bags lined with kid leather were perfect for tobacco pouches. The vogue for the reticule lasted until the early twentieth century.

During the second half of the nineteenth century, many commercially-made reticules were available. In Germany, beautiful beaded reticules were made of Bohemian glass while the Italians prided themselves with their fine

GOLD POCKET WITH BELT.

THIS pocket is intended to hold gold, jewelry, and similar articles, and will be found very useful in travelling. The original is made of a double piece of linen sixteen inches long and eight inches wide; the top is cut slightly convex, while the bottom is rounded. In the middle of the upper piece, cut a slit five inches and a half long, beginning about three inches from the top. Work the edges of the slit in buttonhole stitch with red cotton. Work the edges of the pocket in the same manner, putting the

needle through the double material of the pocket. Bind the top of the pocket between the linen band, in doing which, catch the end of a red cord ten inches long, the other end of which is attached to an oval ring drawn over the pocket. For this ring take three pieces of bonnet wire, and over them work button-hole stitches with red cotton. A brass ring worked in single crochet may be used instead. Sew hooks and eyes to the belt for fastening.

BAG TO BE BRAIDED ON VELVET OR CASHMERE.

GOLD braid on velvet, or cerise on black cashmere, are both pretty.

To those who are unacquainted with the method of transferring the designs to velvet, or any dark material, it would be as well to say that the pattern should be drawn on thick paper, then carefully pricked. Then the pattern should be laid over the material to be worked, and some powdered starch or whitening rubbed over it; on removing the pattern, the design will be traced in white spots, which are then to be followed out with a camel's-hair pencil and white lead.

A belted traveling pocket made of linen. *Godey's Lady's Book.*

Instructions for transferring a design on velvet to construct a braided reticule. *Godey's Lady's Book.*

examples made of Venetian glass. From France came quality bags displaying an Oriental embroidery technique known as tambour work, while magnificent petit point and tapestry bags came from Austria. Although these bags were not factory manufactured in the modern sense of the word, they were made in multiples in small cottage workshops and craft guilds that specialized in specific techniques, and the majority of the work was done by hand. Shops in England sold reticules made from Morocco leather in addition to prime examples made with ivory, tortoiseshell and ormolu (gilded bronze) frames.

In the late eighteenth century, the miser's purse came into vogue. Also called a ring, long or stocking purse, this bag was designed primarily to hold money. Used by both men and women, this elongated bag was knitted, crocheted or netted with silk thread and decorated with beads, fringe and tassels. The beadwork was generally of cut steel but other examples were made with glass beads, gilt beads and even seeds. The purses' opening was located in a narrow section of unbeaded fabric positioned between two larger sides. Two metal rings, sometimes called "sliders", made of steel, silver, gilt, gold or mother of pearl would be pushed down on each of the sides after the coins were deposited. This allowed for their safe keeping. Occasionally,

Evening bag displaying tambour work and chenille embroidery with ormolu jeweled frame and long double chain handle.

HARVARD TOBACCO POUCH.
Gray Silk No. 1164, with Flags, Star, Cord, and Tassels of Harvard Crimson Corticelli Purse Twist No. 1061.

Tobacco pouch, circa 1903.

Back view of Austrian Petit Point handbag.

Front view of Austrian Petit Point handbag with jeweled frame.

Two Miser's Bags made of brown purse silk with cut steel beadwork and long twisted bead tassel, European.

Two Miser's Bags made of purse silk with cut steel beadwork and fringe on one and cut steel beadwork and ring mesh fringe on the other, both American made.

Unusual Miser's purse made of chocolate brown purse silk with white seed bead ornamentation and two Mother of Pearl sliders.

Two miniature hand made purses with steel frames, short chain handles and steel beaded tassels.

Victorian coin purse, nickel plate with embossed leaf and grape design, cloth lined with divided interior, short metal chain for hand carrying.

miser's bags were designed with one rounded end and one squared end so that the user could determine different coins in each side of the bag. This design aided the user traveling at night when lighting was deficient. Eighteenth century examples are larger than those constructed in the nineteenth century. There appears to be no difference, however, between those made for men or women.

In September of 1862, *Godey's Lady's Book* featured directions for making a miser's purse in open crochet. They appeared in the Juvenile department of the magazine with the heading'' Articles that children can make for Fancy Fairs, or for Holiday Presents.'' What a delight to find a child today who would be capable of executing such a task!

By the 1880s, popularity for miser's purses slowly diminished as commercially-made leather coin purses became available. But needlework magazines continued to carry them until the early twentieth century. This slender bag was conveniently designed to be worn over the belt, although in later decades it was twisted around the finger and carried in that manner until its demise.

A slight variation of the miser's purse was a colonial purse constructed with two distinct sections of knitted or crocheted silk. The colonial purse was attached to a metal frame and chain handle which was usually made of steel. Popular throughout the nineteenth century, the colonial purse was used into the first decade of the twentieth century.

By the last quarter of the nineteenth century, industrially-produced goods were in evidence in all areas of fashion. Manufacturers advertised purses, pocketbooks and handbags in hundreds of styles, materials and price ranges. The popularity of machine-made articles rose while the need for hand-crafted items began to decline. An exception was the work of a few individuals involved in the Arts and Crafts movement led by William Morris. Commercially-made products were less expensive than hand-crafted ones and readily available through mail-order catalogues and large department stores.

Small metal purse with embossed designs, cloth lined and three inside compartments.

JUVENILE DEPARTMENT.

Articles that Children can make for Fancy Fairs, or for Holiday Presents.

LONG PURSE IN OPEN CROCHET.

Materials.—One French skein of fine claret silk, and eight of gold thread, No. 1; two rich tassels, and slides to correspond.

The peculiarity of this purse is, that whereas close or single crochet is used, almost invariably, when two or more colors are worked together, in this specimen the open crochet only is employed.

With the claret silk make a chain of 132 stitches; close it into a round, and work three rounds in open square crochet.

1st Pattern round.—* 4 dc with the gold, 2 chain with the silk * repeat all round. Observe that in this and all subsequent rounds, in which both materials are employed, the thread of the one not in use must be concealed within the one that is. Thus the gold thread is to be worked into the chain, as well as the silk into the gold dc.

2d.—Like the first, the 4 dc coming over 2 chain and one dc on each side of it.

3d.—Open square crochet, in silk.

4th.—* 1 dc, 2 ch, silk ; 4 dc gold ; 2 ch, 1 dc, 2 ch silk,* repeat all round.

5th.—* 1 dc, 2 ch, silk ; 7 dc gold ; 2 ch silk, * repeat all round.

6th.—* 4 dc, gold ; 2 dc, silk ; * repeat all round.

7th.—* 7 dc, gold ; 2 ch, 1 dc, 2 ch silk ; * repeat all round.

8th.—* 1 dc, 2 ch, silk ; 7 dc, gold ; 2 ch, silk ; * repeat all round.

9th.—* 1 dc, gold ; 2 ch, 1 dc, 2 ch, 1 dc, 2 ch, silk ; 3 dc, gold ; * repeat all round.

10th.—Like 5th.

11th.—Like 7th.

12th.—Like 6th.

13th.—Like 5th.

14th.—Like 4th.

15th.—All silk, open square crochet.

16th and *17th.*—Like 1st and 2d.

Do eight rounds of open square crochet with silk, then 1 gold, 5 silk, 1 gold, 5 silk, 1 gold, 8 silk. This forms the centre of the purse.

For the other end, repeat from the first pattern round, and after the 17th finish with 2 rounds of open square crochet in silk.

Sew on the tassels, and slip on the slides.

There is so little work in this purse, that it is particularly suitable for any one who wishes to prepare an elegant present in a hurry.

MISCELLANEOUS AMUSEMENTS.

Game of the Two Crosses.

Take thirteen counters and arrange them in the form of a cross, as in Fig. 1. Count your perpendicular line and you will find *nine*. Then begin at the bottom, count seven, and turn to the right, you will find *nine* again ; repeat this and turn to the left, you will still find *nine*. Now take *two* counters away from the thirteen, arrange them in a cross, so they may still count nine each way.

Fig. 1.   Fig. 2.

The solution is, take one counter from each arm of the cross, and move the remaining counter of each arm one counter higher up, as in Fig. 2.

The Cook who Doesn't Like Peas.

The leader of the game puts the following question to the assembled players in succession :—

"My cook doesn't like peas ; what shall we give her to eat?"

A player suggests "turnips," "potatoes," "a piece of bread," "chops," "a penny roll," "pork," etc.

To all these, the questioner replies, "She doesn't like them (or it)—pay a forfeit."

Another proposes "carrots," "dry bread," "beef," "mutton," etc., the answer to any of which is—

"That will suit her," and the *questioner* pays a forfeit.

If only two or three are in the secret, the game proceeds for some time to the intense mystification of the players, who have no idea what they have said to incur or escape the penalties. It depends upon a play of words. The cook not liking "*P's*," the player must avoid giving an answer in which that letter occurs. As the same proposition must not be repeated twice, those even who are in the plot are sometimes entrapped ; the answer they had resolved on being forestalled by another player, they have no time for consideration.

Instructions for making a long purse (Miser's) featured in *Godey's Lady's Book* in 1862.

Colonial purse made of silk decorated with steel beads.

Miniature leather coin purse with short chain handle, gilded base metal frame, hand monogrammed in script lettering.

Large purse made of black silk moire' with sterling silver frame marked GORHAM, off-white watered silk lining. *Her Own Place.*

Purses made of plush, (a silk or cotton fabric made with a long and even pile and soft texture), were very much in vogue in the 1880s. Plush closely resembled fur without the expensive price tag. Genuine fur purses and muffs were also fashionable at this time. Pouch-shaped purses, made of black velvet mounted on sterling silver frames with chain handles, were the height of fashion. The frames were richly engraved or ornately embossed being exceptionally stylish for evening wear. Occasionally the velvet body of the bag was further embellished with cut steel or jet beads.

Handbags, purses and pocketbooks were skillfully made of leather with hand-tooled or embossed designs. The frames also were embossed, the sides were gusseted for a roomy interior, the linings were fancy and durable, the bottoms were sometimes fringed and they were available with strap or cord handles. Knob clasps and slide closures were common on handbags and purses of this vintage.

Manufacturers imported a host of purses, handbags and pocketbooks made of genuine animal and reptile skins from all over the world. Calfskin, seal, walrus, lizard, alligator and crocodile were a few of the most popular. Morocco leather, (which is goatskin tanned with sumac to produce a firm yet flexible leather enriched by a unique pebble grain), had been a favorite for centuries. Imitation Morocco leather, termed "Roan", was often made of sheep or lambskin. Another favorite by costly choice was Russia leather, made of a variety of different skins, recognized by its dark spots and pleasant odor of birch. Imitations had also become popular and priced accordingly.

In the 1880s, alligator leather was all the rage. Various shaped bags offered for sale from Bloomingdale's consisted of handbags, small opera bags, club bags and satchels. Only slight variations of size and shape accounted for the different names of the bags. They were all linen-lined with nickel locks and clasps. Prices ranged from thirty-nine cents to $5.19 depending on the size of the bag and the workmanship involved in its construction. Because alligator leather was so popular, other pliable leathers such as goatskin were grained to produce the alligator effect. In doing this, manufacturers were able to offer an alligator imitation at fractions of the cost of the genuine skins. Although leather handbags, purses and pocketbooks were made in abundance, very few have survived the test of time. These bags were literally used until they completely wore out and eventually were discarded.

Miscellaneous Tourists' Articles.

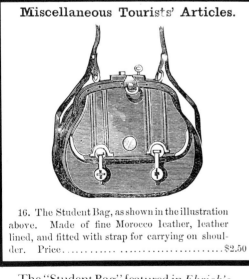

16. The Student Bag, as shown in the illustration above. Made of fine Morocco leather, leather lined, and fitted with strap for carrying on shoulder. Price...............................$2.50

The "Student Bag" featured in *Ehrich's* in 1879.

Traveling Bags.

16. Split Leather Bag, with outside pocket, and nickel trimmings; linen lined. Prices: 9 in., 90c.; 10 in., $1.00; 11 in., $1.10; 12 in.,...............$1.20

17. The same as No. 16; leather lined. Prices: 9 in., $1.15; 10 in., $1.40; 11 in., $1.60; 12 in.,....1.85

18. Black Grain Leather Bag, with outside pocket and nickel trimmings; leather lined. Prices: 9 in., $1.40; 10 in., $1.65; 11 in., $1.90; 12 in., $2.15; 13 in.,.............................2.40

19. The same as No. 18, in Red or Brown. Prices: 9 in., $1.65; 10 in., $1.90; 11 in., $2.15; 12 in., $2.40; 13 in.,.............................2.65

Traveling bag featured in *Ehrich's Fashion Quarterly* in 1879.

No. 118. Flat Leather Bag, with inside and outside pockets, leather lined; with turned corners, nickel frame and knob clasp. Black only. Price, $1.50.

No. 119. Very fine Flat Leather Bag, outside pocket; corners faced with fine calfskin; heavy nickel frame and knob clasp. Black only. Price, $1.75.

No. 120. Handsome Calfskin Flat Bag, turned corners, stitched edge, with grain leather front-piece; outside pocket, nickel frame and knobs. Black only. Price, $2.50.

Three leather handbags featured in *Ridley's Fashion Magazine* in 1882.

No. 115. Seal Leather Pocketbook, with handle; nickel inside frame and clasps. Well made and durable. In red, black or brown. Price, $1.50.

No. 116. Ladies' Pebble Leather Flat Bag; nickel frame and knob clasp, with pocket inside and embossed leather front-piece. Black only. Price, $1.00.

Two leather handbags offered for sale in 1882.

Top—Envelope style calling card case made of genuine alligator with silver ornament positioned over snap closure. Bottom—Leather coin case with nickel frame embossed with Roman coins.

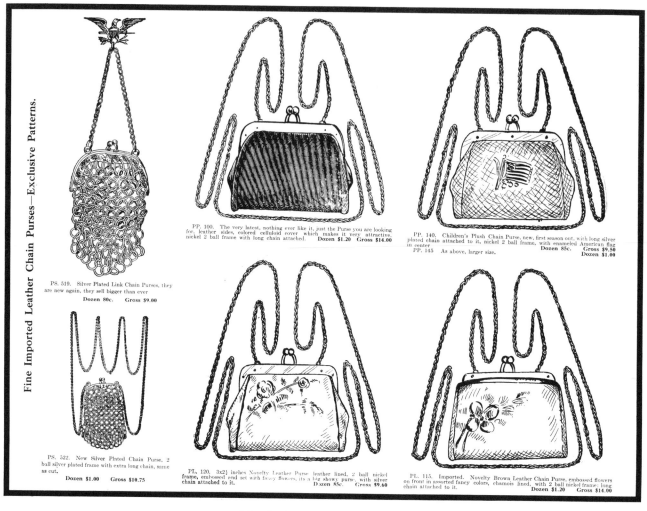

Fine Imported Leather Chain Purses—Exclusive Patterns.

PS. 519. Silver Plated Link Chain Purses, they are new again, they sell bigger than ever
Dozen 80c.   Gross $9.00

PS. 522. New Silver Plated Chain Purse, 2 ball silver plated frame with extra long chain, same as cut.
Dozen $1.00   Gross $10.75

PP. 100. The very latest, nothing ever like it, just the Purse you are looking for, leather sides, colored celluloid cover which makes it very attractive, nickel 2 ball frame with long chain attached.   **Dozen $1.20   Gross $14.00**

PL. 120. 3x2½ inches Novelty Leather Purse leather lined, 2 ball nickel frame, embossed and set with fancy flowers, its a big showy purse, with silver chain attached to it.   **Dozen 85c.   Gross $9.60**

PP. 140. Children's Plush Chain Purse, new, first season out, with long silver plated chain attached to it, nickel 2 ball frame, with enameled American flag in center.   **Dozen 85c.   Gross $9.50**
PP. 145   As above, larger size.   **Dozen $1.00**

PL. 115. Imported. Novelty Brown Leather Chain Purse, embossed flowers on front in assorted fancy colors, chamois lined, with 2 ball nickel frame; long chain attached to it.   **Dozen $1.20   Gross $14.00**

Metal ring mesh and leather chain purses offered for sale from M. Gerber Company.

Top—Gatetop expansion frame, ormolu filigree set with imitation amethyst stones; Bottom—Gatetop frame, nickel plated with engraved designs.

Pocketbooks and handbags of this vintage had up to ten inside compartments intended for calling cards, tablets, pencils, puffs, handkerchiefs, opera glasses, fans and mirrors besides the actual billfold which was designed for paper money. These pocketbooks and handbags for women were designed to hold everything and more than what a man could carry around with him in his thirteen pockets! This was achieved without distorting the figure since bulges were still considered a sign of bad taste. As a result, handbags for women achieved high popularity.

The gatetop or expansion purse frame which came into vogue in the 1880s created a novelty sensation. Constructed with a metal folding gate collar and a round flip top, the frame expanded when opened. The body was usually made of silk, brocaded velvet or tapestry, but metal ring mesh became a preferred choice in the 1890s. The round metal top was often elaborately engraved, embossed, filigreed or jeweled. To close the bag, the metal gate is pushed back together and the flip top snapped back in place. Cloth or chain handles were attached for hand carrying.

Soft chamois leather was used frequently in early purses with double nickel frames and it is found as a lining material in other leather purses. Flat bags made of heavy-grained leather called "Ladies' Pebble Bags" had nickel frames, occasionally with inside and outside pockets and knob clasps. For

Open view of gatetop expansion frames.

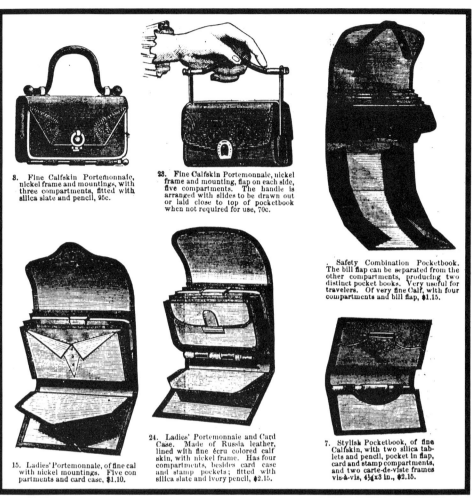

8. Fine Calfskin Portemonnaie, nickel frame and mountings, with three compartments, fitted with silica slate and pencil, 95c.

23. Fine Calfskin Portemonnaie, nickel frame and mounting, flap on each side, five compartments. The handle is arranged with slides to be drawn out or laid close to top of pocketbook when not required for use, 70c.

. Safety Combination Pocketbook. The bill flap can be separated from the other compartments, producing two distinct pocket books. Very useful for travelers. Of very fine Calf, with four compartments and bill flap, $1.15.

15. Ladies' Portemonnaie, of fine cal with nickel mountings. Five con partments and card case, $1.10.

24. Ladies' Portemonnaie and Card Case. Made of Russia leather, lined with fine écru colored calf skin, with nickel frame. Has four compartments, besides card case and stamp pockets; fitted with silica slate and ivory pencil, $2.15.

7. Stylish Pocketbook, of fine Calfskin, with two silica tablets and pencil, pocket in flap, card and stamp compartments, and two carte-de-viste frames vis-à-vis, 4¼x3 in., $2.15.

A variety of small pocketbooks featured in *Ehrich's* in 1880.

Black Pebble grain leather handbag with leather strap handle. Multiple frames with three separate knob clasps opening into three separate sections containing a total of seven inside compartments and added coin purse. Frame marked GRIP-TITE JEMCO.

No. 103. Calf Pocketbook, with handle and tastily embossed front piece. Brown, red or black. Price, 57c.

No. 107. Fine Calf Pocketbook, with handle and bird enameled lock, nickel inlaid frame. Colors, red and black. Price, 80c.

Pocketbooks offered for sale in 1880.

Combination pocketbooks and card cases offered for sale in 1895.

No. 100. Ladies' fine Calf Pocketbook, with covered nickel frame, tablet and pencil. In red, brown or black. $1.13.

No. 104. Calfskin Pocketbook, with heavy nickel top frame and cord and tassel. Red, brown or black. Price, $1.00.

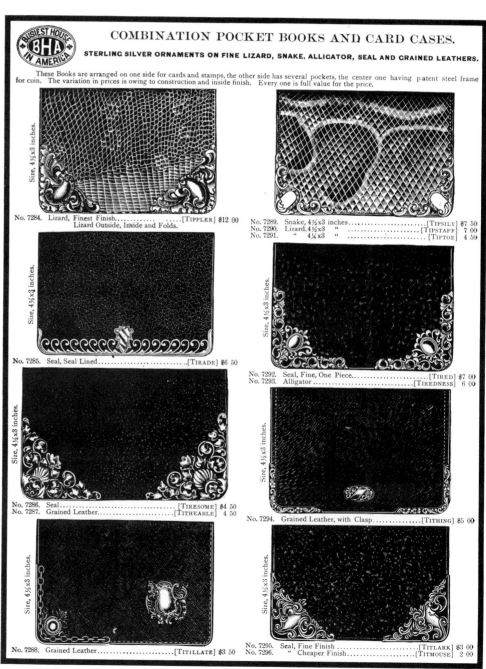

COMBINATION POCKET BOOKS AND CARD CASES.

BUSIEST HOUSE IN AMERICA BHA

STERLING SILVER ORNAMENTS ON FINE LIZARD, SNAKE, ALLIGATOR, SEAL AND GRAINED LEATHERS.

These Books are arranged on one side for cards and stamps, the other side has several pockets, the center one having patent steel frame for coin. The variation in prices is owing to construction and inside finish. Every one is full value for the price.

Size, 4½x3 inches.

No. 7284. Lizard, Finest Finish............[TIPPLER] $12 00
Lizard Outside, Inside and Folds.

Size, 4½x3 inches.

No. 7289. Snake, 4½x3 inches.............[TIPSILY] $7 50
No. 7290. Lizard, 4½x3 " ....[TIPSTAFF] 7 00
No. 7291. " 4¼x3 " ....[TIPTOE] 4 50

Size, 4½x3 inches.

No. 7285. Seal, Seal Lined.............[TIRADE] $6 50

Size, 4½x3 inches.

No. 7292. Seal, Fine, One Piece.............[TIRED] $7 00
No. 7293. Alligator ....[TIREDNESS] 6 00

Size, 4½x3 inches.

No. 7286. Seal.............[TIRESOME] $4 50
No. 7287. Grained Leather.............[TITHEABLE] 4 50

Size, 4½x3 inches.

No. 7294. Grained Leather, with Clasp.............[TITHING] $5 00

Size, 4½x3 inches.

No. 7288. Grained Leather.............[TITILLATE] $3 50

Size, 4½x3 inches.

No. 7295. Seal, Fine Finish ....[TITLARK] $3 00
No. 7296. " Cheaper Finish.............[TITMOUSE] 2 00

women who were in a state of full mourning, "Ladies' Mourning Pocketbooks" were available in black calfskin, lined with black watered silk. If the pocketbook had a metal frame, it too was enameled black. Real jet or black glass (called French Jet) was used extensively at this time as a garniture for clothing as well as accessories.

Safety combination pocketbooks were also popular and they were constructed in a way that the bill flap could be separated from the other compartments producing two different pocketbooks. Advertised as being useful to the traveler, combination pocketbooks were made of calfskin and they retailed for $1.15 in the 1880s. A small pocketbook called a *portemonnaie* was designed to hold coin and currency. It was fitted with five or more inside compartments, a silica slate and pencil.

Sentimental and souvenir purses were fashionable throughout the nineteenth century. The sentimental nature of Englands' Queen Victoria inspired manufacturers and craftsmen to design jewelry and accessories full of sentimental inscriptions. Little coin purses charmingly constructed of large "bivalve" shells were decorated with floral designs or sentimental inscriptions hand painted directly onto the shell. Often, they were attached to small chain handles. These shell purses are very characteristic of the second half of the nineteenth century and continued to be stylish right into the twentieth century. Phrases like "From a Friend", "My Heart is Yours", "Loving Heart Purse" and "My Sweetheart Purse" graced these little Victorian treasures. They were perfect for gift giving or bought as seashore souvenirs.

Small bivalve shell purse with short chain handle.

Shell and leather souvenir purses offered for sale from M. Gerber Company.

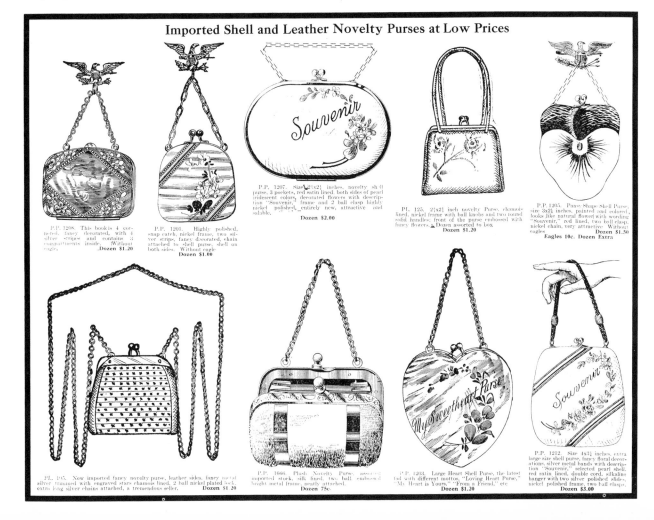

Imported Shell and Leather Novelty Purses at Low Prices

P.P. 1208. This book is 4 cornered, fancy decorated, with 4 silver stripes and contains 3 compartments inside. (Without eagle.) Dozen $1.20

P.P. 1201. Highly polished, snap catch, nickel frame, two silver strips, fancy decorated, chain attached to shell purse, shell on both sides. Without eagle. Dozen $1.00

P.P. 1207. Size 2¼x2¼ inches, novelty shell purse, 3 pockets, red satin lined, both sides of pearl iridescent colors, decorated flowers with description "Souvenir," frame and 2 ball clasp highly nickel polished, entirely new, attractive and salable. Dozen $2.00

Pl. 125. 2¼x2¼ inch novelty Purse, chamois lined, nickel frame with ball knobs and two round solid handles; front of the purse embossed with fancy flowers. ⅓ Dozen assorted to box. Dozen $1.20

P.P. 1205. Fancy Shape Shell Purse, size 3x2¼ inches, painted and colored, looks like natural flower with wording "Souvenir," red lined, two ball clasp, nickel chain, very attractive. Without eagles. Dozen $1.50 Eagles 10c. Dozen Extra

Pl. 195. New imported fancy novelty purse, leather sides, fancy metal silver trimmed with engraved stars chamois lined, 2 ball nickel plated lock, extra long silver chains attached, a tremendous seller. Dozen $1.20

P.P. 1666. Plush Novelty Purse, assorted imported stock, silk lined, two ball embossed bright metal frame, neatly attached. Dozen 75c.

P.P. 1203. Large Heart Shell Purse, the latest fad with different mottos, "Loving Heart Purse," "My Heart is Yours," "From a Friend," etc. Dozen $1.20

P.P. 1212. Size 4x3¼ inches, extra large size shell purse, fancy floral decorations, silver metal bands with description "Souvenir," selected pearl shell, red satin lined, double cord, silkaline hanger with two silver polished slides, nickel polished frame, two ball clasps. Dozen $3.00

Sovereign case made in the shape of a pocket watch with two inside compartments; one side has reverse painted scene while the opposite side reveals a watch face.

Sovereign purses, characteristic of the English gold coins they were designed to carry, were small purses made of leather, suede or metal. Sometimes smaller than an inch in diameter, these coin purses were used throughout the nineteenth century. Metal sovereign cases were occasionally made to look like lockets or small pocket watches. They were decorated with hand painting, engraving, embossing and enameling.

In 1889, leather novelty folding coin purses were patented by The James S. Topham Company. Advertised as the sole manufacturer of this type of purse, they were made of dyed Morocco leather, full calf and genuine seal, retailing for forty-, seventy-, and ninety-cents respectively. Nineteen years later, Sears, Roebuck and Company offered the "Paragon Patent Folding Coin Purse" which looked exactly like its nineteenth century counterpart. This purse was made of "Morocco finished leather." The description in the catalogue stated that "this purse will hold $10.00 in silver." It was made to lie flat in the pocket and at the same time will prevent coins from falling out. It sold for twenty-four cents.

"Trick Purses" were popular around 1900. Nothing more than a little leather framed coin purse, this item became instantly popular because of its

Small sovereign case, silver plated with embossed design of a woman, Pat'd. 1903; Finger ring coin case, souvenir of Lexington Park, inside fitted with two coin holders.

Monogrammed coin case with attached chain handle, inside fitted with three coin compartments, marked German Silver.

Silver sovereign case made like a small pocket watch with fluted designs. *John Morse Jr..*

trick clasp. Patent combination locks were used with instructions given on the correct way to open this purse. Other features included a nickel riveted frame, a chamois lining and one or more inside compartments. They were made of buckskin and kid leather. The M. Gerber Company, located on South Street in Philadelphia, distributed leather trick purses for as low as eighteen cents a dozen.

Evidence from early catalogues and fashion journals informs us that handbags, purses, pocketbooks or whatever term a manufacturer would suggest became an integral part of the fashion scene towards the end of the nineteenth century. This functional accessory was not only an excellent receptacle for carrying personal and necessary items but it also was used to add the finishing touch to complete the overall costume. Besides the manufactured variety, many were artistically created in the home for personal use or gift giving. In America, *Godey's Lady's Book* was crammed full of fancy work instructions for making reticules, miser's bags, watch pockets and much more which inspired women from all walks of life to create these accessories themselves. Many of the homemade accomplishments, which were lovingly passed down for posterity, can be found today.

See additional advertisements for early handbags on pages 161 and 162.

SHOPPING BAG.
Bag is about 6 inches each way, with hook for belt, Kid Lined, with Pocket.

No. 7310. Lizard....[TOLERABLE] $12 00
No. 7311. Seal.....[TOLERATION]   7 50
Silver Name Plate.

Shopping bag offered for sale in 1895.

Top—Tam O'Shanter coin purse with crocheted bottom decorated with steel beads. Bottom—Coin purse, embossed frame made of nickel plate over brass, knob clasp. *Christine Ketchel.*

Sterling silver finger ring purse, English hallmarks. *Her Own Place.*

Fine Boston Bag

FOR shopping, motoring, short visits, week-ends and many other occasions every woman needs a Boston bag. Men, too, find them equally as useful. The one offered here is made of long wearing, genuine cowhide, strongly sewed throughout, color brown, fully lined, and with a large, roomy side pocket. It fastens with a leather strap and buckle. The leather handles are not only sewed to the sides but also firmly riveted to the metal frame, thus rendering them doubly strong and capable of standing the heaviest strain. This bag is of good size, measuring 14 inches in length, 9½ inches high and 6 inches wide at the bottom, and it is really surprising to see what a lot of things you can get into it. When ordering, please mention Gift No. 2461.

Given for Six Subscriptions

Fine leather Boston Bag given as a free premium for magazine subscription.

Chatelaine made of sterling silver with
attached mesh gatetop purse, mirror,
pencil, shoe buttoner (marked
Germany) and vanity case, circa 1890.

Chapter II:

❧ The Chatelaine Bag

In November of 1911, Louise Willis Snead wrote an article entitled *Dainty Handbags for Home Making* which appeared in *McCall's Magazine*. The following is an excerpt from that article:

> "One frequently hears the modish gown likened to the picturesque costumes of the Renaissance, and as frequently one hears mention of the term 'Moyen-age.' The phrase takes one back some three or four centuries to the middle ages and the feudal castle. The wife of the baron was called the chatelaine, or lady of the castle; from the effigy in bronze above her resting-place, we of today picture her in semi-fitting princess robe, the square neck filled in with lace 'modestie,' and a jewelled girdle encircling her waist. Emblematic of her station the keys of her great storerooms hang suspended from this girdle—likewise the quaint purse; her bone needles for lace-making and her gold ones for the interminable tapestry weaving are also attached for convenience. In the inevitable evolution of dress, receptacles were gradually introduced—pouches or reticules—to carry all these things, and their highest development was the chatelaine bag, so artistic and exquisite in workmanship and design that all subsequent periods have adopted and copied this essentially feminine and housewifely article. And so today in reproducing the princess gown of Guinevere or Beatrice, or of the noble Venetian and Florentine ladies, the medieval costume would be incomplete without the bag. Today milady carries her keys and purse, her handkerchief and 'vanity box' in a reticule so necessary that it has become a part of her costume—and a different one for every costume is gaining favor with all well-dressed women."

Ms. Sneads' article paints a vibrant picture of the medieval castle and the baroness or chatelaine. The name, originally applied to the person, later corresponded to the object, hence the chatelaine became an ornamental hook that was worn at the waist. Attached to this hook were numerous chains attaching implements such as sewing items, watches, pomanders, patch boxes, notebooks, pencils, seals, keys, stamp cases and scent bottles which dangled conveniently. The original medieval practice evolved into a revival appendage which proved useful as well as fashionable.

In the eighteenth century, costly solid gold chatelaines, enriched with precious stones, carved cameos and delicate enamel work were fashionable among the upper class. They became popular for gift giving, especially wedding presents for a bride. In the nineteenth century, less expensive examples were made of pinchbeck, a material which resembled gold. Sterling silver, cut steel, oxidized silver, gilt and brass chatelaines were also common throughout the nineteenth century. Victorian women enjoyed wearing this lavish and culturally romantic accessory. It proved to be useful especially during periods when reticules were slightly outmoded, particularly in the 1840s and again in the 1870s. In the interim, however, evolving fashion, creating impetus for new accessories, put the medieval chatelaine bag into the limelight once more. Although the basic idea behind the bags construction had existed for centuries, it was not until the nineteenth century that the term "chatelaine bag" was actually used.

Chatelaine bag made of German silver flat mesh with ornate embossed frame marked "Warranted German Silver". The inside of this bag contained a small sheet of paper which read: "Bought and given to Anne by Murdo McPherson, Dad's cousin and at that time Murdo was Canada's Attorney General."

In 1863, the English fashion magazine, *Queen*, commented on chatelaine bags:

> "For some time past chatelaine bags have been very popular in England. They have been worn at the side suspended to the waistband. These have generally been made of leather and studded with steel, and for traveling have been found very convenient. For home wear they are made of gimp or embroidered velvet."

Although chatelaine bags were popular in England at that time, they were first seen in Paris a few years earlier.

By the summer of 1879, an American publication known as *Ehrich's Fashion Quarterly* advertised chatelaine or belt bags made of genuine alligator and calf leather accompanied by a belt and braided chatelaine hook. Brocaded silk chatelaine bags were also featured with nickel frames, satin linings and filigreed chatelaine hooks. Plain leather chatelaine bags were frequently called "Shopping Bags."

In 1882, *Queen* again commented on the importance of this modern accessory:

> "Pockets in skirts are still impossible for if they contain anything beyond the finest of handkerchiefs they bulge and make themselves ungracefully apparent. The result is that the chatelaine bags are adopted by those who may require to carry card-case and purse besides the necessary handkerchief, for as the spring wears on the convenient muff-bags must be dispensed with."

Chatelaine bag made of black velvet, ornate 800 silver frame with Cupids and castle motifs, marked NG. The frame is actually a double frame; once opened, a center frame is visible with two inside compartments. This center frame is marked AN. The inside of the bag is lined with black silk. This bag is possibly of German origin. *Her Own Place.*

Vinaigrette with attached finger ring, silver plate over copper openwork design, accented with blue medallion.

Silver plated vinaigrette with embossed design and openwork pattern.

Vinaigrette and chatelaines featured in *Ehrich's* in 1879.

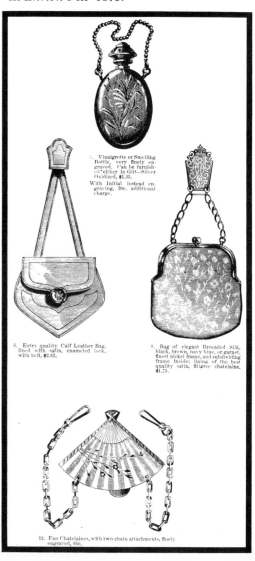

Chatelaine bag with ornate nickel-plated frame and crocheted rings of black silk forming beehive pattern, silvered bead fringe, circa 1905. *Her Own Place.*

Circular chatelaine bag made with jet beads that were silvered which completely cover the front surface of the bag. The back of the bag is made of chamois with a chamois lining. The flower motif frame is nickel-plated.

In 1886, Bloomingdale's offered buckhorn leather chatelaine coin purses only large enough to hold a few coins. They were constructed with braided leather chains and hooks retailing for seventy-nine cents. More elaborate examples, made of brass or gilded base metals, were often filigreed and set with imitation stones.

In 1895, The Montgomery Ward Catalogue displayed a variety of genuine grained leather chatelaine bags. One example was made of black lizard grained leather which contained an oxidized metal frame, a nickel-plated chain and chatelaine hook. This bag sold for twenty-five cents. Other examples mentioned were made of Vienna calf and seal-grained leather. The seal-grained bag was designed with a flap and an oxidized metal clasp; it was called a "Cleopatra Bag."

Chatelaine coin holder made of brass in openwork pattern enriched with green paste stones.

Late nineteenth and early twentieth century opulence created a wonderful aura of elegance and sophistication which made the chatelaine bag an indispensable accessory. Alexandra, wife of England's King Edward VII, dictated contemporary taste and revived the use of a chatelaine, so fashionable women from all walks of life followed her lead.

In the early part of the twentieth century, just like centuries before, women's thrift and abilities in hand work prompted them to save scraps of material, lace, net, spangles, beads, buckles, brocades, chenille, bullion and artificial jewels in cases which were referred to as "treasure boxes." Little would be discarded and it was said that nearly everything came back in style every seven years. Instructions were given in Ms.Sneads' article (*McCall's Magazine*, November, 1911) to construct chatelaine bags with the scraps of material and garnitures saved in treasure boxes. One example that was mentioned was an oriental chatelaine bag made of heliotrope velvet lined with lilac taffeta. The bag was to be decorated with Persian embroidery made in a raised design and further embellished with artificial turquoise stones and spangles. This bag was specifically intended to be worn with a heliotrope broadcloth evening gown.

Other hand-crafted examples were assembled with scraps of furniture brocade and a loop and button fastener with added tassels. In addition, velvet, kid, satin, cretonne, chintz, moreen, pompadour ribbons, corduroy, pongee, watered silk and canvas were also put to use as chatelaine bag materials. Creativity was expressed with an endless amount of trims. For example, beads, lace, soutache braid, fringe and tassels were abundantly utilized. Different hand work techniques such as embroidery, applique and crochet were prominent. Hand-painting, stenciling and piping were also frequently evidenced on bags of this vintage.

Manufacturers and importers offered many styles of frames and hooks and a wide range of materials were utilized for their construction. For example, sterling silver, oxidized silver, German silver, silver plate, nickel plate, gunmetal, steel, aluminum, brass and gilt chatelaine frames and hooks were quite common. Other materials included gold filled, rolled gold plate, ribbon and leather. The wealthy society belle, preferring expensive chatelaine bags made of solid gold, could commission such an extravagant item from a fine jeweler or goldsmith. This type of bag is rarely, if ever, found today.

Chatelaine bag fashioned with French jet beads on one side and black velvet on the other side, nickel silver embossed frame and hook. The inside is lined with chamois.

Three silver chatelaine hooks, repousse' designs, Pat'd. Feb. 11, 1902.

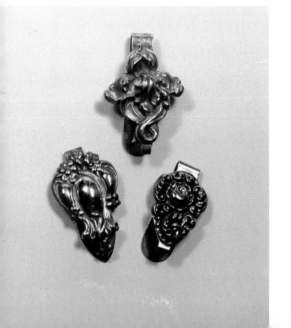

Chatelaine purse top made of silver gilt in filigree design and set with imitation turquoise stones cut *en cabochon.*

Besides the tremendous variety of materials, the designs were also plentiful. Motifs such as flowers, butterflies, ladies, bows, Cupids, fans, sporting themes and *fleur de lis* were common. Filigree and openwork patterns were fashionable in addition to heavily engraved or embossed designs. The frames were skillfully crafted and extremely ornate being very characteristic of the late nineteenth and early twentieth centuries.

The chatelaine hook was attached to a small metal ring about ½ inch in diameter. Suspended from this small ring two chains made the connection between the hook and the purse frame.

Commercially-made examples of the purse body were made of leather, chamois, velvet, plush and metal ring mesh. Beading was extremely fashionable usually in the form of French or American cut steel beads or French jet beads that were silvered; the latter being the less expensive variety. Colored glass beads were also employed on early French chatelaine bags as well as English and American examples. Very few bags of this kind, however, are found today. When leather, suede or chamois was used to make the bag, the front of the bag was completely encrusted with cut steel beadwork while the back of the bag was often left plain. This makes a lot of sense considering the way the bag was worn with only one side facing out as opposed to a bag that was hand-carried with both sides visible.

MIRROR FOR POCKET OR CHATELAINE.

Cut Full Size.

This oval mirror with *fleur de lis* ornamentation sold for $2.50 in 1895.

Rolled gold plate chatelaine hooks popular in 1895.

ROLLED GOLD PLATE CHATELAINES.

No. 920. Each....$1 75
Hard Soldered Wire,
Assorted Patterns.

No. 921. Each..$2 25
Hard Soldered Wire,
Assorted Patterns.

No. 922. Each.$2 75
Polished Stone Set.
No. 923. Each.$4 00
Enameled.

No. 924. Each.$2 00
Roman Open Work.

No. 925. Plain..........................Each $1 00
No. 926. Assorted Chased.............. "   1 00

Round chatelaine bag made of American cut steel beads and bead fringe. The back of the bag is crocheted in beige silk, chamois lined, nickel plated frame and chatelaine hook.

American made circular chatelaine bag made of jet beads that were silvered with beaded fringe, nickel-plated frame, marked Pat'd. Feb 7, 1900.

In the last quarter of the nineteenth century, black velvet, plush and satin were used in abundance for chatelaine bag making and the majority of these bags were mounted on heavy sterling silver frames that were exceedingly ornate. Repousse' work was also stylish at this time with motifs such as Cupids, flowers and birds which appear on many examples. Makers' marks, dates and sometimes inscriptions can be found on the frame helping to date a particular example. Careful observation of the chatelaine hook can also prove helpful.

In the 1890s when metal ring mesh had created a dramatic impact on purse making, lovely chatelaine bags were also made of this material. Woven wire chatelaine bags were also made with spring-hinged tops which were decorated with large brilliant cut stones. They were advertised as the latest novelty in 1899.

A purse that is characteristic of the 'Gay Nineties' is the finger ring purse. Structurally similar to the chatelaine bag, the ring purse was made with a much larger ring than that attached to the chatelaine bag. This larger ring, connected to either one or two chains, would then connect to the frame of the purse, which was usually constructed of metal mesh. This ring would conveniently fit on the finger and the purse would be carried in that fashion. Most ring purses, manufactured in varying qualities of metal ring mesh, assumed smaller proportions than chatelaine bags.

ROUND CHATELAINE BAG No. 11.

Round chatelaine bag fashioned with a continuous circular pattern of cut steel beads and additional beaded fringe.

Chatelaine purse made of chain work on nickel silver, circa 1895.

654 **Nobby Chatelaine Purse—** Latest novelty, woven **wire** purse, heavy embossed pattern, spring hinged lid, set with large brilliant cut stones in colors, ring and chain to suspend from belt, heavy gold-plated Roman finish, each put up on a handsome printed card. Per dozen............ **$3.25**

Chatelaine purse made of woven wire with jeweled top offered for sale from Lyon Brothers in 1899.

Finger ring purse made of armor mesh, marked 925 Sterling, with repousse' work on frame. *John Morse Jr.*

Contemporary mini chatelaine bag made of electroplated woven metal mesh. *Amber Lee Ettinger.*

Finger ring purse made of armor mesh with embossed frame, marked German Silver.

Edwardian woman carrying finger ring chatelaine, circa 1910.

Round chatelaine bag made of flat metal mesh in circular pattern, frame and hook both marked German Silver displaying heavily embossed designs.

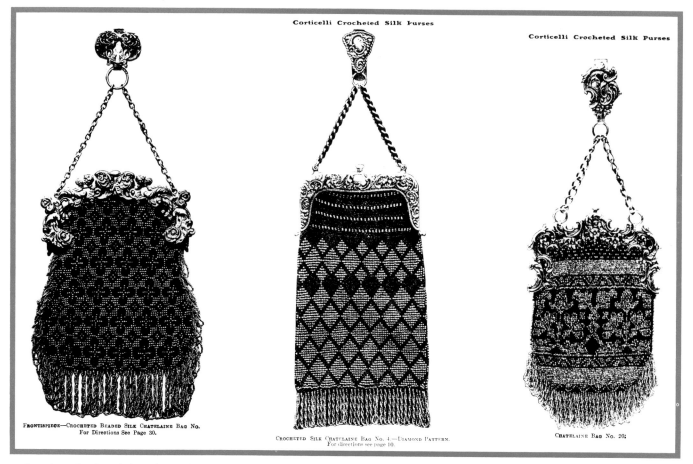

Corticelli Crocheted Silk Purses

Corticelli Crocheted Silk Purses

FRONTISPIECE—CROCHETED BEADED SILK CHATELAINE BAG No.
For Directions See Page 30.

CROCHETED SILK CHATELAINE BAG No. 4—DIAMOND PATTERN.
For directions see page 10.

CHATELAINE BAG No. 20;

Crocheted chatelaine bag decorated with steel beads and ornate German silver frame and hook, circa 1900-1905.

Chatelaine bag crocheted with steel beads in diamond pattern attached to an oxidized silver frame.

Chatelaine bag made of silk purse twist, steel beads and ornate embossed frame and matching chatelaine hook.

Crocheted chatelaine bag with steel bead fringe and embossed nickel-plated frame and chain handle.

By the turn of the century, a revival in crochet fancy work lent itself nicely to lovely homemade chatelaine bags. Numerous pattern books were available. The Corticelli Silk Mills of Florence, Massachusetts published small guides with instructions for making chatelaine bags out of Corticelli Purse Twist, a three-cord thread. Black and white engravings accompanied each set of instructions which provided a detailed look at the finished product accented with steel, gilt or glass beads. The purse twist was available in many new shades made specifically for chatelaine bags and small coin purses, especially the Tam O'Shanter. Colors like Lily grey, crimson rose, seal brown, bronze green, nile green, scarlet, garnet and canary were mentioned.

Finer silk was used for fringe, so that old beaded bags found today, often are in need of fringe repair. This finer silk was basically not strong enough to support the weight of the beads over long periods of time.

Many varieties of crocheted chatelaine bags with bead ornamentation were made using No.8, No.9 and No.10 commercial beads. Round chatelaine bags, completely encrusted with steel beads and looped fringe, about 4½ inches in diameter, seem to have been the most plentiful since they are easily obtainable today.

Curiously enough, since chatelaine bags had become so popular, other articles were manufactured in the chatelaine style. For example, spectacle cases, attached to ornamental hooks were available in 1895. Bon bon or

Crocheted chatelaine bag made of chocolate brown purse silk and jet bead ornamentation, nickel plate over brass frame with embossed designs.

Bon Bon Box attached to chatelaine hook, circa 1895.

Spectacle cases with attached ornamental chatelaine hooks, circa 1895.

This memo tablet with pencil attached to *fleur de lis* chatelaine hook was popular in 1895.

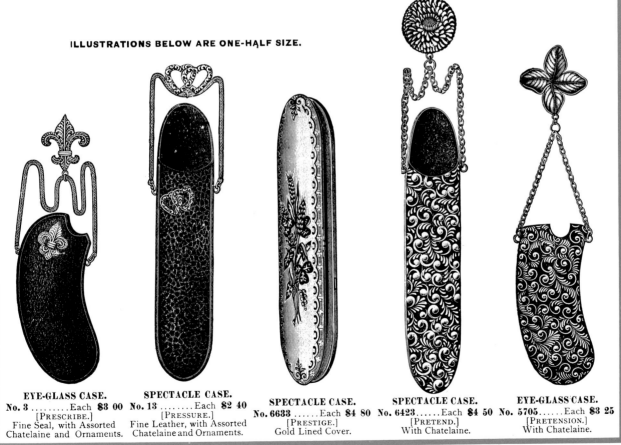

ILLUSTRATIONS BELOW ARE ONE-HALF SIZE.

EYE-GLASS CASE.
No. 3 ....Each **$3 00**
[PRESCRIBE.]
Fine Seal, with Assorted
Chatelaine and Ornaments.

SPECTACLE CASE.
No. 13 ....Each **$2 40**
[PRESSURE.]
Fine Leather, with Assorted
Chatelaine and Ornaments.

SPECTACLE CASE.
No. 6633 ......Each **$4 80**
[PRESTIGE.]
Gold Lined Cover.

SPECTACLE CASE.
No. 6423......Each **$4 50**
[PRETEND.]
With Chatelaine.

EYE-GLASS CASE.
No. 5705......Each **$3 25**
[PRETENSION.]
With Chatelaine.

Ladies' Fancy Metal Chatelaine Purse in Nickel or Silvered.

No. 18R2649 The design is a reproduction of the high priced all silver purse. Chain and belt hook to match. This is a very dainty and elegant purse. Size, 3x5 inches. Price, each............75c
If by mail, postage extra, 6 cents.

Ladies' Genuine Alligator Chatelaine Purse.

No. 18R2651 With fancy metal frame, ball catch, chain and attachment for belt. Size, 4½x4¾ inches. Price, each..........$1.25

If by mail, postage extra, 10 cents.

Chatelaine Bags.

No. 18R2653 Seal Grain Leather Bag. One leather lined pocket, gilt riveted ball catch frame, gilt chain with attachment for belt. Size, 3x3½ inches. A very convenient and pretty bag.
Price, each............23c
If by mail, postage extra, 6 cents.

Ladies' Chatelaine Bag.

No. 18R2655 Ladies' Seal Grain Leather Chatelaine Bag. With nickel riveted frame, the front of frame covered with leather, patent nickeled catch fastener, leather straps and belt hook. Size, 6x6½ inches.
Price, each............46c
No. 18R2657 Ladies' Chatelaine Bag, similar shape to above, made of finest real seal, leather lined, best frame. A substantial wearing as well as elegant bag. Black only.
Price, each....................$1.00
If by mail, postage extra, each, 8 cents.

Black Leather Chatelaine Bag.

No. 18R2691 Black Leather Chatelaine Bag. Imitation walrus, riveted frame with leather front, spring catch, one regular and one outside handkerchief pocket; wide bottom and sides. Size, 5¾x6¼ inches. This is an exceptionally fine, stylish book and exceptional value.
Price, each...............95c
If by mail, postage extra, 8 cents.

Chatelaine bags made of metal and leather offered from Sears in 1902.

mint boxes, made of quadruple plate, fashioned in the form of flowers, were also attached to chatelaine hooks and worn at the waist. Memo tablets with attached pencils were suspended from decorative hooks as well as calling card cases attached in the same manner. Fan chatelaines were popular in the early 1880s made of oxidized silver or gilt with delicate engraving.

By 1902, The Sears, Roebuck Company offered numerous chatelaine bags through their mail-order catalogue in a wide variety of styles, materials and price ranges. Their most expensive bag, made of genuine cut steel beads, had steel beaded fringe, a chamois lining and a silver-plated frame, chain and hook. Available in a small and large size, this bag retailed for $3.29 and $4.95 respectively. At the other end of the market, their chatelaine bags made with links of silver-finished white metal sold for forty-nine cents each. Sears also offered chatelaine bags in genuine alligator, seal or imitation walrus.

Towards the end of the nineteenth century, a 'new woman' emerged who relied on practical garments for outdoor activities and lavish fashions for evening wear and social gatherings. Her new attire lent itself to the use of chatelaines and chatelaine bags. From medieval appendages, the form evolved to become an integral part of the ''modern'' costume of every well-dressed woman.

See additional advertisements for chatelaine bags on page 163.

Crocheted chatelaine bag decorated with steel beads attached to silver-plated frame, inside lined with chamois, American.

Ladies' Cut Steel Beaded Bags.

They have become more and more stylish. Every lady wants one.
No. 18R2637 Beaded Bag. Genuine hand made, cut steel beaded bag, with steel bead fringe, chamois back and handsome silver plated frame, chain and hook, chamois lined and inside pocket. Very stylish; all the go. Size, 4x4½ inches. Price, each....$3.29
If by mail, postage extra, 10 cents.
No. 18R2639 Hand Made Beaded Cut Steel Bag. Same style as above but larger. Size, 5x4½ in.
Price, each....................$4.95
If by mail, postage extra, 12 cents.

Ladies' Fine Beaded Chatelaine Purse.

No. 18R2643 Made of steel beads and looped fringe all around, chamois lined, chain and belt hook. A very handsome bag at a very low price. Size, 4½x6¼ inches. Price, each............$1.50
If by mail, postage extra, 10 cents.

Ladies' Steel Bead Chatelaine Purse.

No. 18R2645 Mounted handsomely with fine nickel frame, chain and belt hook attachment, beaded loop fringe all around, chamois lined. This purse is usually retailed at $1.50. Size, 4x4¾ inches. Price, each.........................$1.00
If by mail, postage extra, 8 cents.

Novelty Metal Chatelaine Bags.

No. 18R2647 Made of fancy links of white metal, silver finish, with chain belt hook. A very stylish purse. Size, 2½x3¼ inches.
Price, each. 49c
If by mail, postage extra, 5 cents.

Cut steel and ring mesh chatelaine bags offered from Sears in 1902.

Chapter III

❧ Early Twentieth Century Handbags

New and attractive handbags and purses were advertised everywhere at the turning of the new century. Handbags became necessary and "important features of fashionable dress." Different bags were designed for each season, special occasions and even specific times of day. A bag used in the afternoon when invited for tea was not appropriate for an evening at the opera. Leather bags were preferred for shopping excursions while large carpet and tapestry bags were more suitable for traveling. "Motor bags" were specifically designed for traveling by car and "Railway bags" were still quite fashionable when traveling by train. Those bags considered in the "best taste" were usually made simple yet pleasingly elegant. Novelty handbags were now only appealing if they contained fittings that were useful. The inside of the bag was equally important and careful thought was given by craftsmen and manufacturers when designing fitted handbags.

Antelope leather handbag attached to ornate silver-plated frame with Cupid motifs. This frame was originally attached to a much earlier bag.

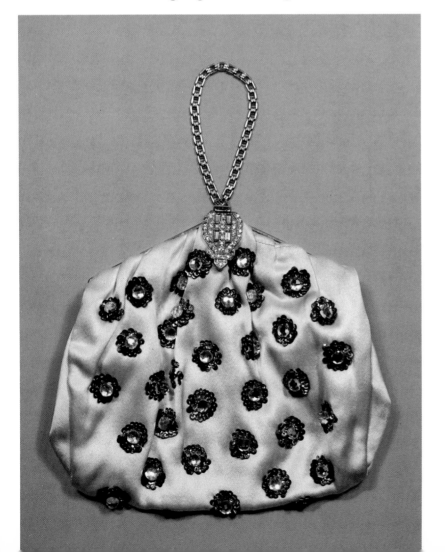

Silk evening bag ornamented with rhinestone studs and sequins, jeweled lift lock and short chain handle.

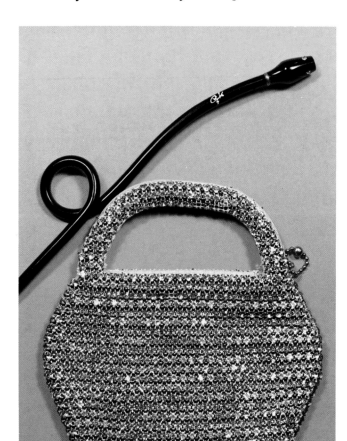

Bakelite cigarette holder made in the shape of a snake. Rhinestone top-handled evening bag with zippered closure, grosgrain lining with label that reads: "Made In Czechoslovakia", circa 1930s.

Egg-shaped Edwardian coin purse made of German Silver with engine turned designs attached to a 30-inch chain embellished with faceted crystal stones.

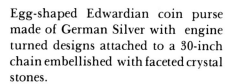

Unusual celluloid link handbag made to resemble tortoiseshell with double black silk cord handles and black celluloid beads used as sliders to hold down or lift open the lid of the bag.

Women preferred to buy a bag to match their costume just as a century before when it was preferred to make one. Leather, for example, could be professionally dyed to match a suit, dress or coat. Other handbag materials included silk moire', crepe de chine, brocaded velvet, satin, cretonne and tussahs. Morocco leather handbags continued to be fashionable in addition to those made of suede. Handbags made of "duvetyn" were unique to this period. Duvetyn was a new material that possessed a suede-like quality without the genuine suede price tag. Purses made of black velvet were worn with "costumes of all colors." For evening wear, black velvet purses were further embellished with cut steel beads in rather simple patterns which added just enough sparkle to be appropriate. Velour purses with added worsted embroidery were also stylish at this time. The bodies of the handbags were often hand-painted, stenciled, braided or embroidered with silk. Oxidized ornaments, gilded clasps, marcasites and gemstones were common garnitures that enriched these lovely handbags and purses of the early twentieth century.

Suede handbag displaying cut-leather work, circa 1909.

Black silk velvet handbag, geometrically decorated with tiny cut steel beads, silk lined, marked K & G Charlet Bag, Paris, New York.

Burgundy velvet handbag with sterling silver and marcasite lift lock. The frame of the bag is also covered with velvet but the inside frame is left plain and marked Jemco.

Purple satin envelope style bag decorated with hand blown glass balls, leaves and ribbons, snap closure. *Her Own Place.*

Misses' Sea Lion Grain or Suede Bag

Given Free for a Club of Only Two Yearly Subscribers at Fifty Cents Each, or Four at Forty Cents Each ✦

Premium No. 359 is a very attractive bag made of a good quality of sheepskin leather, in the sea lion grain, lined with figured moire and containing an inside purse made of the same leather. The Vienna handle is the latest and best, and this bag is equipped with one. The bag measures 7 inches at its widest point, and is 4½ inches deep, exclusive of handle. It has a 5-inch nickel frame, with nickel ball and clasps. It is offered only in black.

Premium No. 360 is a new style of bag offered to our patrons this season for the first time. It is made of suede, which is the soft side of the leather, and makes a very odd and pretty bag. It is lined with moire, and has a Vienna handle. It is 6⅛ inches long at the widest point, and is 3¾ inches deep, exclusive of handle. It has a 5-inch gilt frame, with ball clasps. It can be supplied in either brown or gray. Mention color when ordering. We will send either Bag, as above described, by mail post-paid, also THE LADIES' WORLD for one year, upon receipt of only **Eighty-five Cents**; or we will give either Bag *free* to any one sending us a club of **Two** subscribers for one year at 50 cents each, or **Four** subscribers at 40 cents each. Or we will send either Bag post-paid, without subscription to the magazine, upon receipt of 45 cents.

No. 359

No. 360

Ad from *The Ladies' World*, circa 1906.

Silk brocade back strap pouch, gilded frame, satin lining, fitted with mirror, comb, coin purse and compartment for lipstick and powder compact.

Russia Bag made with Mole Plush trimmings, circa 1917.

Gold kid leather evening bag, enameled frame, lift lock closure, satin lining marked Made in France.

Double framed cloth back strap pouch with jeweled lift lock.

Seal Grain Bag With Embossed Frame

Given Free for a Club of Only Five Yearly Subscribers at 50 Cents Each, or Ten at 35 Cents Each

This is a handsome bag of generous proportions, made of genuine leather, and a very much finer article of its kind than anything we have offered in former years. The frame is beautiful, being embossed with a conventional floral design and silver-plated in the French gray finish. The bag measures 10¼ inches in length, and 7¼ inches in height, not including the leather handle. It is lined with moire, and contains an inner pocket fitted with a small leather coin purse. It is made of first quality material throughout and has ample capacity for holding every small article that a lady is accustomed to carry. Our illustration shows its general shape which is a very popular one. We know the bag will please any lady who becomes its fortunate possessor. Our broad guarantee of absolute satisfaction or money refunded covers this bag as well as every other one of our premiums. We know this bag will please all who select it. We will send the Seal Grain Bag with Embossed Frame above-described by mail post-paid, also THE PEOPLE'S HOME JOURNAL for one year, upon receipt of **$1.60**; or we will give the Bag *free* to any one sending us a club of **Five** subscribers for one year at 50 cents each, or **Ten** subscribers at 35 cents each. Or we will send the Bag post-paid, without subscription to the magazine, upon receipt of $1.25.

The Peoples' Home Journal, November, 1911.

The Triad, "A Club or Society Bag for Young Girls", circa 1917.

"Richelieu" embroidered handbag, circa 1910.

The exquisite fashion taste of this opulent era enabled many women to indulge in extravagant fur accessories. Coats, hats, collars, cuffs, scarves, muffs and handbags were beautifully fashioned from "furs of the newest mode." Fox, ermine, raccoon, mink, seal, skunk, monkey, beaver, muskrat, pony and wolf were some of the most popular. Women carried fur muffs in conjunction with fur handbags. Occasionally, the muff was treated like a handbag since it contained hidden pockets or compartments for personal belongings. Large muff-bags had been available since the 1880s, but by the early twentieth century extravagant use of furs was an understatement; a few women even wore genuine fur robes to lounge around the house. Furs became the epitome of elegance and sophistication during the period 1901-1910.

Expensive furs also were imitated in less expensive furs. For example, black fox, which was a costly favorite, was simulated by dyeing raccoon or skunk. "Hudson seal" was nothing more than "French dyed" muskrat. This practice enabled average women to feel and look as elegant as their wealthier friends.

Ermine collar, muff and handbag, circa 1911.

Many purses and handbags of this period were imported from Europe, especially Paris, which had been the fashion center for many decades. Newest styles in French handbags were quickly available in America. Sixteenth century-style Venetian cut-work was utilized for "Novelty" bags sold in exclusive Paris boutiques. This type of medieval needlework was renamed "Richelieu" embroidery in this new century and became a fashionable hobby for women who still enjoyed creating their own handbags and purses at home. Handbags decorated with tambour work also were plentiful.

Handbags made of brightly-colored taffeta, trimmed with Valenciennes lace, were stylish as well as homemade reticules of colorful silk ribbon, either plain or printed. Bags of striped antelope leather (a deep brown color resembling brown chamois) were seen in the first decade of the twentieth century. Because of its soft texture, it was sometimes called "velvet suede." Buffed calf skin bags were also appealing because of their "soft mottled effect and dull finish."

Small wrist bags of cross stitch embroidery on canvas were fashionable in the first decade of the twentieth century. The patterns for beaded bags were adapted slightly so that the cross stitch could be substituted for the beads. Striking designs using silk flosses in various shades were thus rendered creating illusions of miniature tapestry bags. Instructions were frequently found in needlework magazines with emphasis that stitches be worked in the same direction so the pattern would be even. Beaded wrist bags were also popular with floral or scenic designs on light and dark backgrounds.

In 1903, crochet and embroidery were recommended to relieve stress and other ailments that did not require "pills and potions." One eminent physician of the period gave his opinion of fancy work in the *Chicago Chronicle*:

"I am using fancy work quite extensively in my practice and with even greater success than expected. I have several women patients taking it, and their gain in mental and physical tone is marked...Tranquilize the spirit and the body responds. If a sufferer from nervous prostration can be induced to forget herself even for a brief time each day, it means much toward recovery."

Draped Colonial Bag, circa 1917.

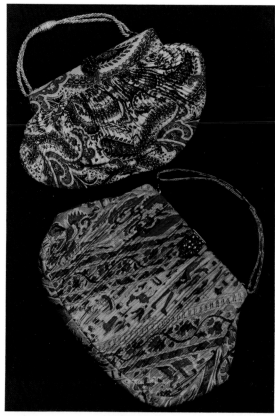

Two pleated cloth handbags with brass frames and lift lock closures, Middle Eastern influences, circa 1920.

Hand crocheted drawstring reticule popular in the early Twentieth century.

WRIST BAG NO. 3.
Sprays of White Blossoms worked with Corticelli Roman Floss on Tan Canvas.

Wrist bag worked in cross stitch, *Home Needlework Magazine*, July, 1903.

Pleated cloth bag, bright colored fabric, jeweled lift lock closure, cord handles, silk lined with inside pocket fitted with small mirror.

Petit Point Handbag with jeweled frame further embellished with enamel ornamentation, Made In Austria. *Her Own Place.*

Top—Needlepoint bag in floral design with black border, framed in brass with twisted wire chain handle. Bottom—Needlepoint bag with black background and floral motifs and enameled frame.

Petit Point Handbag with pearl and enamel frame, classical scene with watered silk lining. *Her Own Place.*

Brown needlepoint handbag with floral theme, jeweled frame and ornate chain handle, grosgrain lining with two shirred pockets. *John Morse Jr..*

Needlepoint bag, floral motif, ornate jeweled frame with bezel-set imitation stones and jeweled clasp and double chain handle. Late Nineteenth Century.

Woven Tapestry bag.

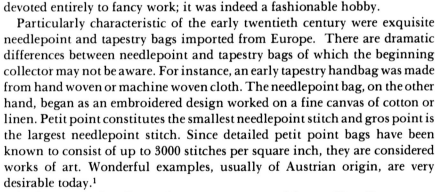

Almost every woman's magazine of the period included special sections devoted entirely to fancy work; it was indeed a fashionable hobby.

Particularly characteristic of the early twentieth century were exquisite needlepoint and tapestry bags imported from Europe. There are dramatic differences between needlepoint and tapestry bags of which the beginning collector may not be aware. For instance, an early tapestry handbag was made from hand woven or machine woven cloth. The needlepoint bag, on the other hand, began as an embroidered design worked on a fine canvas of cotton or linen. Petit point constitutes the smallest needlepoint stitch and gros point is the largest needlepoint stitch. Since detailed petit point bags have been known to consist of up to 3000 stitches per square inch, they are considered works of art. Wonderful examples, usually of Austrian origin, are very desirable today.[1]

Early tapestry handbags often were constructed from still earlier tapestry wall hangings or other early cloth. A tapestry bag framed in the nineteenth century could have been an eighteenth century cloth. Others pieces of tapestry, however, were designed specifically for handbag use. Accurately dating bags like this is difficult. The best method is checking the frame for hallmarks or manufacturer. Early frames are ornate and frequently garnished with real gemstones, paste imitations, seed pearls, enamel and filigree work. They were made from solid gold, pinchbeck, sterling silver, silver gilt, brass and electroplated base metals. The chains which suspend the early bags are heavier, longer, and more elaborate than later ones and sometimes doubled. Once a date for a frame has been established, the date of the body of the bag can still be questionable.

---

[1] A detailed study of needlework handbags can be found in *More Beautiful Purses*, by Evelyn Haertig, an invaluable reference book on purses.

Figural design Tapestry handbag (front) with gilded frame and satin lining, marked Made In France.

PETIT POINT BAGS

specially priced

32.00 to 115.00

these imported masterpieces, known for their fine quality workmanship and choice designs, are being offered to you at the lowest prices in history. Exquisite bags that make a lasting gift . . . that every woman treasures . . . An array of gorgeous patterns copied from famous tapestries found in the foremost art galleries of Europe . . . in soft, rich colorings, each an outstanding work of art entailing thousands of hand-worked stitches . . . thousands of colors. Various sizes and shapes, mounted on frames of filigree work, set with enamel, pearls and stones.

Every Petit Point Bag is specially priced for this event

Bags   *First Floo*

Petit Point Bags offered for sale in December of 1930 at Bonwit Teller in Philadelphia.

French Tapestry handbag displaying back view.

Large Tapestry bag with leather handle, floral theme on both sides, nickel frame and watered silk lining.

Rare Imported
Petit Point Bags
An Exquisite Group Just in From Vienna

Needleworkers who formerly wrought for royalty made these matchless *petit point bags*. Like real laces and diamonds, they are heirloom possessions Floral and figure designs in the soft colors of antique Gobelin tapestries . . . the needlework so miraculously fine that it seems almost like a woven fabric. Mounted on jeweled frames, they are among the loveliest gifts you could send the bride of June . . . or the bride of many years! $75 to $250.

Petit Point bags offered for sale in June of 1930 from John Wanamaker of Philadelphia.

The motifs on early tapestry and needlepoint bags are significant in reflecting social, historical and intellectual aspects of the original needleworker. Inspirations were drawn from literature, sculpture, painting, woodcuts and engravings. Embroidered representations can be found depicting classical, biblical, mythological, pastoral and floral themes. The results were exceptional handbags which are highly prized today.

By the second decade of the twentieth century, especially during World War I, women who wanted fancy goods were somewhat forced to resort to their handwork skills, and therefore their skills continually improved. Crocheting was enjoyed by young and old and many crocheted purses found today date back to this period in time. Scores of pattern books had dozens of examples in each issue. With so many different patterns to choose from, each bag was given a specific name. For example, the "Mandarin Bag" was a large wrist bag constructed with thirty spools in eight colors of crochet silk, satin cloth and Chinese wrist rings for handles. The "Saddle Bag" was made with eleven spools of crochet silk, two bunches of mercerized coronation cord, ½ yard of satin and ½ yard of China silk. This pattern created a stunning wrist bag designed to be worn with a white summer lawn dress. The "Opera Glass Bag" utilized seven spools of crochet silk in two shades of blue to create a smart little pouch for opera glasses.

The Mandarin Bag, circa 1917.

Other bags were given similar names to correspond with their finished appearance. For instance, the "Lantern Bag", made with wine, cadet blue and gold-colored crochet silk, with a touch of black satin, created a bag that looked like an oriental lantern. The "Parachute Bag", made with alternating rows of multi-colored crochet silk, resembled a parachute with a tassel. The "Fleur-de-lis Bag" was a crocheted reticule with a drawstring and *fleur-de-lis* pattern in contrasting color which completely encircled the bag. An earlier version of this bag, made around 1905, has glass beads in the same pattern.

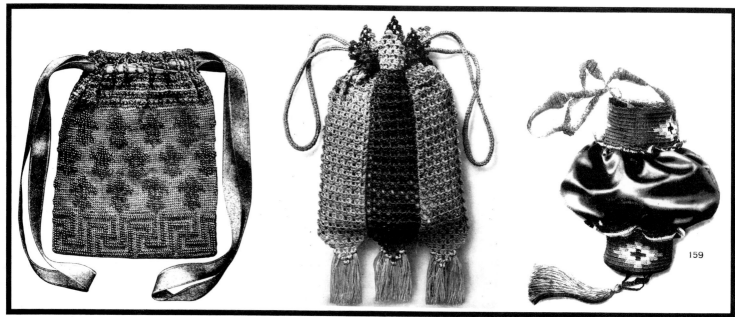

Fleur-de-Lis Opera Bag made of purse silk and gilt glass beads.

Crocheted drawstring reticule, circa 1917.

The Lantern Bag, circa 1918.

Saddle bag in tatting and crochet, circa 1917.

Crocheted bags became extremely stylish for summer and evening wear. Both Irish and Venetian crochet was utilized, with the latter being easier to construct. A combination of these stitches were sometimes employed in the same bag, with Irish crochet on one side and Venetian crochet on the other. Crystal beads could be crocheted right into the pattern creating a more dramatic bag for evening wear. Most often, these bags were made in the reticule style with a drawstring closure in light colors, particularly white, off-white and beige. These bags proved to be appropriate choices for the romantic and feminine dresses of the period.

Gold and silver lace or netting was also used extensively at this time to create expensive-looking evening bags at home. Italian filet work, a type of crochet made to resemble lace, was another favorite technique. Needlework had become so popular that many midsummer vacation days were spent by groups of women "gathered together on verandas or under shady trees" skillfully making wonderful handmade items for personal use and gift giving.

In Paris around 1910, the double-hinged purse frame became popular; when it opens, it forms a square. This was not a brand new style but after it was shown in Paris, it quickly became fashionable in America. Watered silk, brocaded velvet and tapestry were utilized to make up these capacious bags.

The gatetop or expansion purse frame, which came into vogue in the 1880s, also continued to be used in the early twentieth century. Sears offered an "Opera Shopping Bag" in 1902 made of black moire' silk with a gatetop frame and silk cord handles. In the late twenties, Sears still carried gatetop framed handbags with tapestry bottoms, but by this time they were referred to as "gatetop purses."

Double-hinged frame.

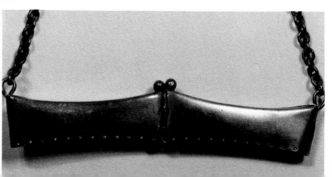

Open view of double-hinged frame showing how this mechanism forms a square.

Large tapestry bag, figural design, attached to nickel-plated double-hinged frame.

Large brocade bag attached to double-hinged frame.

Floral Tapestry bag attached to double-hinged frame.

Double purse frame with Cupid motifs attached to cord handles, Nineteenth Century.

Handbags made with more than one frame were also common and very practical. Multi-framed bags gave manufacturers the option of including many inside compartments which women still loved. Most of these bags were constructed with the inner frame attached to the same hinges as the outer frame. A small coin purse was usually put on the inner frame at the center forming compartments on each side.

Paris dress designers considered it "imperative for fashionable dress" that the bag match the costume whenever possible. Designers would take a piece of cloth matching the garment, garnish or embroider it and have it sent to a purse manufacturer for finished frame. The frames tended to be rather large. Women who used these bags carried them under their arms in an "inverted position grasping the chain handles and metal frame."

Frameless reticule-style handbags, made of colored silks, were cleverly constructed with a little round mirror set into the bottom of the bag. They were said to be "more easily and unobtrusively consulted than a chatelaine or purse mirror." This novelty was very useful, but its popularity was short-lived.

A chiffon velvet handbag made by Colonial Hand Bags of New York City and called "The Nassau" was also practical with a tiny mirror placed on the reverse side of a beaded flap. It also contained a change purse which was nestled "securely in a shirred pocket." In 1917, this purse retailed for $15.00.

Metallic gauze, a material first used in the 1820s, became stylish around 1910. Used over colored silks, satin or mouselline, this type of gauze fabric possessed an unusual luster which resembled precious gems. Fancy reticules made of metallic gauze were favored for evening wear with bead embroidery using imitation stones resembling coral, turquoise, lapis lazuli and chrysophrase.

Vanity topped gatetop expansion frame marked German Silver.

Metallic gauze handbag with chenille floral embroidery, gilded frame marked Made in France. The inside of the bag is lined with silk and contains a shirred pocket and round mirror. *Christine Ketchel.*

Shoulder bags became the rage in the second decade of the twentieth century. Ironically, shoulder bags were not necessarily carried on the shoulder; when cord handles were extremely long they were wound around the wrist or knotted and hand carried. Frequently, two or more shoulder bags were carried simultaneously, a small shoulder bag being used for coins while another was designed specifically for calling cards, and a third would be a vanity or opera glass case. This fashion trend possibly evolved from the use of chatelaines and other waist accessories but the liberated woman of the twentieth century preferred to sling everything over her shoulder instead of wearing it around her waist.

Handbag manufacturers well into the twentieth century continued to produce quality bags made of genuine leather as technology improved and more varied leathers were available. Ostrich leather was chic for purse making and manufacturers stated that it was impossible to imitate. Heavily-grained leathers such as hornback alligator, armadillo, snakeskin, lizard, seal, goat and walrus all had attractive grain patterns. Just as expensive furs were duplicated, manufacturers did the same with genuine leather. For example, seal leather was grained to look like walrus; goat was grained to look like seal; and sheepskin was grained in the sea lion motif. Anything technologically possible in the field of duplicating was done to create a greater variety and a wide range of prices for all levels of income. Imitation leather, called leatherette or leatherine, was abundantly made and sold at fractions of the cost of the genuine skins.

Hornback alligator handbag with braided leather handle, lined in pebble grain leather fitted with round mirror.

Ostrich leather handbags, billfolds, key cases, tobacco pouches and cigarette cases offered for sale from the Jason Weiler and Sons 1927 catalogue.

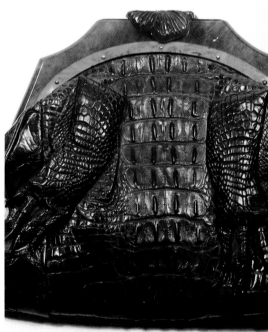

Alligator back strap pouch with Bakelite frame and carved lift lock.

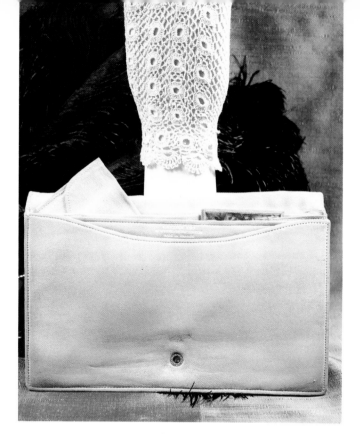

Brown leather bag decorated with embossed metal medallion positioned on leather flap, double frame with inside coin purse.

Antelope leather handbag with Prystal and marcasite lift lock. Inside frame and coin purse are marked "The Aristocrat."

Leather envelope style underarm bag with eight inside compartments lined with silk and fitted with smaller coin purse lined with white kid leather. The inside of the bag is stamped "Cartier Inc. New York—Paris—London, Made In France."

The Boston Store, Chicago, Illinois, circa 1910.

Six-sided suede pouch with drawstring closure enriched with steel bead ornamentation, lined with damask.

The catalogue listings read:

29C6400—Very stylish hand bag, made of selected genuine leather, seal grained; real leather gussets; cave-in bottom; dull silver metal frame, very artistic design; leatherine lined; double real leather handles. 12x8½ inches. Black only. Postage, 23c extra. Price $1.39

29C6401—Elegant hand bag, made of genuine leather, seal grained; Parisian pattern; leather covered frame; excellent lock; genuine double leather handles; leatherine lined; inside pocket, fitted with coin purse; has large outer compartment, with flap; monogram plate clasp. Black only. 13¾x8¾ inches. Postage, 25c extra. Price $1.69

29C6402—Magnificent hand bag of highly selected genuine leather, seal grained; cave-in bottom; real leather gussets; dull silver metal frame made with three fancy imported ornaments, which are attractive; lined with genuine leather; has inside pocket fitted with coin purse; strong double real leather handles. 12x8½ inches. Black only. Postage, 25c extra. Price $1.95

29C6403—Latest novelty in a hand bag, made of extra good quality velvet or satin; silver metal frame, in the most beautiful design; bag lined with good quality fancy material; inside pocket; long double silk cord finished with silk tassels. Black only. Velvet or satin. 11x7½ inches. Postage, 7c extra. Price 94c

29C6404—Latest Parisian strap bag, made of genuine leather; cave-in bottom; real leather gussets; silver metal frame, fancy design; lined with poplin; inside pocket

29C6409—A bargain in a German silver frilled mesh bag; has four silver ball drops; genuine German silver metal frame, made in a very handsome design; bag lined with real white kid; inside change pocket. Made with real white kid. 5½x4½ inches. Postage, 11c extra. Price $1.98

29C6410—Very latest German silver mesh bag, of extra high grade; four silver ball drops. Made with the newest wish bone frame, worked in dainty floral design; lined with real white kid; inside change pocket; chain handle. 5½x5 inches. Postage, 10c extra. Price $3.47

fitted with coin purse, outer compartment with flap; extra long genuine leather strap handle. These bags are now all the rage. 6½x5½ inches. Black only. Postage, 10c extra. Price 98c

29C6405—Very popular mosquetaire bag, made of good quality satin; trimmed all around with imported French novelty braid, 1¾ inches wide; lined with good quality material. Closes with cord as shown; long double silk cord handle. 10½x8½ inches. Black with fancy colored braid. Postage, 8c extra. Price 96c

29C6406—Hand bag, of the very finest selected genuine leather, real seal grained; cave-in bottom; real leather gussets; high grade silver metal frame, beautiful Arabian design; excellent quality genuine leather lined; inside pocket fitted with coin purse; has long strap handle. 10x8½ inches. Black only. Postage, 18c extra. Our special price $1.98

29C6407—Latest creation in a hand bag of the best quality genuine suede leather; silk embroidered on one side, in an artistic design; high grade gold frame, pretty design; lined with silk poplin; inside pocket fitted with coin purse; extra long double silk cord handles. 11x8 inches. Postage, 11c extra. Price $1.89

29C6408—Extra large German silver mesh bag of selected grade; finished with five ball drops; large genuine German silver frame, made in an artistic design; bag lined with genuine white kid; has inside change pocket; finished with chain handle. Double. 7x6¼ inches. Postage, 18c extra. Price $4.98

29C6411—Our special lady's hand bag, made of imitation leather, seal grained; covered frame; good lock; moreen lined; has four pockets, fitted with mirror, coin purse and card case; strong double handle. Black only. 11x8½ inches. Postage, 13c extra. Price 49c

29C6412—Very beautiful hand bag, made of imitation leather, real seal grained; silver colored metal frame, in neat design; moreen lined; inside pocket, fitted with coin purse; strong double handle; bag has outer compartment, lap-over embossed. 11x8½ inches. Black only. Postage, 13c extra. Price 69c

29C6413—Leatherette hand bag, seal grained; fancy silver metal frame; strong double handle; lined with leatherette; broken bottom style; inside compartments, with fittings. 11½x8½ inches. Black only. Postage, 20c extra. Price $1.19

29C6414—Genuine leather hand bag, fine grained; lined with good quality moreen; cave-in bottom style. Size, 12x9 inches; two strong leather straps; inside pocket and purse; compartments on either side. Closes with fancy shield shaped monogram plate. Black only. Postage, 16c extra. Price $1.00

Popular styles in Hand, Strap and Mesh Bags featured in the Chicago Mail Order Company catalogue of 1911.

In 1910, Chicago's Boston Store offered ladies' fitted handbags made of real goat seal leather and seal-grained leather. These bags were equipped with up to five inside pockets, a mirror, smelling salt bottle, change purse, powder puff, powder box and calling card case. The seal-grained bags sold from forty-eight cents to $2.48 depending on the size, while the more expensive goat seal bags retailed for $3.98.

In 1911, Chicago Mail Order Company sold stylish handbags of genuine leather in different grained effects such as seal and walrus. These bags were made with real leather gussets, cave-in bottoms, and metal frames with short leather handles or long strap handles made of knotted silk cord. The bags were lined with poplin, moreen or leatherette. Imitation leather handbags were also available made with embossed designs and ornamental metal frames. Closures consisted of shield-shaped monogrammed plates, knob clasps or slide locks.

LADIES' HAND BAG

No. J27212. Ladies' Handbag, seal grain leather overlapping leather covered frame, strong spring lock, double strap handle. This bag is well lined with three pockets containing purse, smelling salts bottle and mirror. The bag is 11 inches long, 7 inches deep. Exceptionally good value. Price 98c

Fitted handbag offered for sale in 1910 from The Boston Store in Chicago.

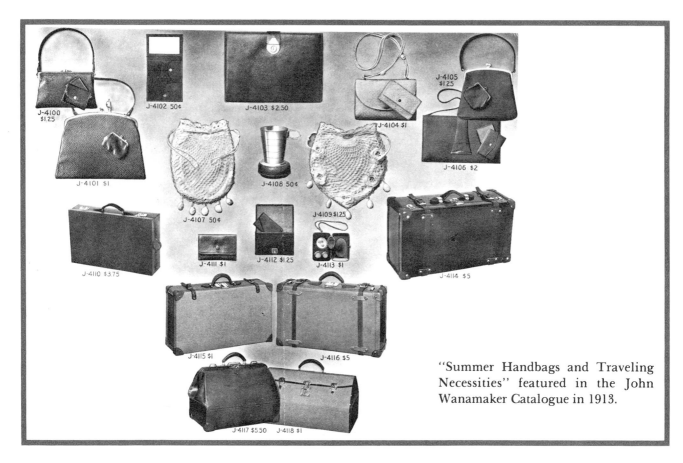

"Summer Handbags and Traveling Necessities" featured in the John Wanamaker Catalogue in 1913.

Hand-tooled leather back strap pouch with Bakelite clasp and gilded copper frame marked JEMCO, Pat'd July 23, 1918. The inside of the bag is lined with green suede and stamped "Justin Leather Goods Co."

Hand-tooled leather bag with wrist strap handle, leather lined stamped "Amity Products." The frame is nickel plated marked JEMCO.

In 1913, John Wanamaker of Philadelphia offered Morocco leather handbags in black, blue, green, Nell rose and tan dyed leather. The frames were made in sterling silver, gunmetal or gilt. A bag of any color or frame combination listed above sold for $1.25.

Hand-tooled leather bags became popular in America around 1900 and continued to be fashionable until the late 1930s. The inspiration for these bags was drawn from medieval craftsmanship and an inherent desire to return to a society not dependent on machines. Handsomely designed in the Arts and Crafts style of free-flowing designs and floral themes, these bags were made of genuine English and Spanish steerhide, cowhide and calf leather. They were made in hundreds of styles and sizes with a short handle or in the flat envelope style to be worn under the arm. Small coin purses, billfolds, vanity bags, cigarette cases and adjustable shoulder strap bags were also made of hand-tooled leather.

Skilled artisans made many of these lovely bags in cottage settings and took pride in their accomplishments. Most of the work was done by hand so they were never referred to as a mass-produced article. The edges of these bags, as well as the handles, were almost always laced by hand with leather.

Elbert Hubbard, a top producer, founded the Roycroft Shops in East Aurora, New York. The Roycrofters, a group of artists completely devoted to hand work in leather, among other items, followed the ideals of the Arts and Crafts Movement initiated by William Morris in England in the late nineteenth century. Hand-tooled leather bags were also produced by Frederick Kranz, founder of Cordova Shops, and H.E.Kaser Modeled Leather Corporation, both located in Buffalo, New York.

Large overnight case made of hand-tooled leather, circa 1930s. *Christine Ketchel.*

Hand-tooled leather top handle pouch, floral design and hand laced edges; Embossed leather billfold hand colored, Pat'd. July 31, 1923.

Hand-tooled leather coin purse, acorn motif, hand laced edges with snap closure.

61816U
$10.00
Size 8 x 7¾ inches

A Gold Plated monogram may be ordered for these Bags at $1.50 additional.

BKS

61816U Ladies' Hand Bag of Brown Spanish hand tooled Leather. This Bag will give long service without showing the wear. Has laced edges and strap handle. Bag is beautifully leather-lined and has removable change purse and mirror. Price..................$10.00

Hand-tooled leather handbag offered for sale in 1927.

Hand-tooled leather handbag as seen in *McCall's*, September, 1908.

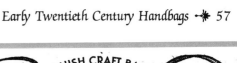

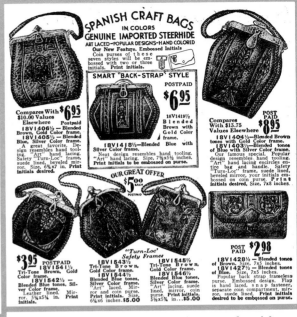

Cameo Genuine English Steerhide Bags advertised in *The Keystone Magazine* September 1929.

Arts and Crafts style bags made with embossed designs sold through the Sears catalogue in 1930.

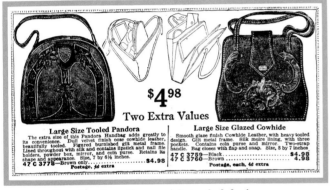

Leather handbags with tooled designs featured in the 1922 Montgomery Ward Catalogue.

Arts and Crafts style bags featured in the Jason Weiler and Sons 1927 catalogue.

As their popularity escalated, other companies began to surface. Worth noting are the Meeker Company (Joplin, Missouri), Springfield Leather Products, Cameo Studios, (Springfield, Ohio), Amity Leather Products (West Bend, Wisconsin), Bosca Company (Springfield, Ohio) and the Justin Leather Goods Company. The bags made by these companies are marked by an embossed initial on the leather or a stamped marking on the inside lining. The majority of their frames were made by an entirely different company known as Jemco. The frames were made of gunmetal, copper or hammered brass and the word "Jemco" almost always appears somewhere on the frame. Bosca Built bags were occasionally enriched with early plastic frames. Naturalistic designs prevailed on these unique treasures which are highly sought after today.

Obviously, not everyone could afford hand-tooled leather accessories. Because of this, factories produced cheaper imitations made of genuine leather with embossed designs resembling the hand tooling. Imitation leather was also available with embossed designs producing similar effects and the edges were often laced with gimp.

Six-sided reticule made of woven straw embroidered with white seed beads and raffia, rope handles and slide closure.

Two Tam O' Shanter coin purses with identical Cupid motif designs on top.

Tam O' Shanter coin purse embossed design of lady on top, steel beaded and crocheted bottom, marked Pat. Dec. 15, 1903.

Tam O' Shanter coin purse crocheted with red purse silk and decorated with steel beads. The top is nickel plated and marked Pat'd. Dec. 16, 1903.

Tam O' Shanter coin purse with steel beaded crocheted bottom and embossed nickel-plated top marked Pat. Mar. 25, 1890.

Raffia, a fiber from the stalks of the Madagascar Palm, had been used for making baskets and hats. In the early twentieth century, raffia was employed as an embroidery thread to contrast the delicate embroidery silks and flosses that were so often used to embellish early fabric handbags. Raffia was generally used on a ground of canvas or burlap producing pouch and drawstring reticules. The designs were simple but unique and they created interesting contrasts to the many accomplishments that women executed in their homes. Silk embroidered bags, however, were more delicate than those made of raffia.

The Tam O' Shanter coin purse was another popular novelty of the early twentieth century. Larger than the earlier nineteenth century sovereign purse, the Tam O' Shanter coin purse had a round crocheted and beaded bottom section which was attached to a round metal purse top. The metal top was most often composed of sterling silver or nickel plate over brass with repousse' or embossed designs. Needlework magazines offered easy to follow instructions for making these little purses at home. The magazines also made it known that the metal purse tops were easy to find at large city stores or direct from importers or manufacturers for a minimal cost.

Prior to the First World War, Americans imported many "fancy" goods from Germany, Austria, France and England. Europe was noted for its manufacture of exquisite articles made in small factories, workshops, guilds or cottage settings. America, on the other hand, was known for its many large factories and its mass-produced articles in quantity; exceptions were those workshops involved in the Arts and Crafts movement in America.

When World War I erupted in 1914, the fashion industry, along with everything else, endured enormous changes in order to economically survive. Although importing and exporting decreased dramatically and designers in both Europe and America had to slow production to a certain degree, they did not completely cease manufacturing the products that the female population desired. Considering the war atmosphere, some felt it "admirable to remain pretty in spite of everything." Some women resorted to being domestic once more. With new concentration on the war effort, most production in Europe switched to manufacturing military uniforms in quantity. Some European designers even fled to America during this period and taught some excellent European manufacturing techniques. As a result of this, manufacturing standards in America began to escalate. With the help of a newly found organization called the Art Alliance of America, designers and manufacturers were guided through extensive industrial art techniques.

When the war was over, manufacturers resumed "normal proportions." America put more effort into the manufacturing process as quality was stressed more than ever. In Europe, mass production techniques were growing with the quality of the product still intact. Europe and America were now much on the same industrial level.

Imposed wartime restrictions created shortages of metal and leather necessary for handbag manufacture. Natural materials, like amber, ivory and tortoiseshell were used for frame construction. At the other end of the market, celluloid and other early plastics were used to create imitations of the natural materials. French ivory, made of celluloid, was common. The plastics could be molded to produce hand-carved effects and they were even tinted with color. In place of leather which had been used tremendously for handbag manufacture, tapestry, needlepoint and beaded bags became the height of fashion.

In December of 1918, *Harper's Bazaar* advertised Christmas gifts through a mail-order shopping service. Many of the gifts were evening bags. Of interest was a brocaded velvet bag with an "antique sterling silver frame and chain." Obviously, the war shortages of metal made it necessary to use older frames on modern handbags. This bag retailed for a costly $68.00. Another bag that was offered was made of black chiffon with an imitation tortoiseshell frame and colored silk lining. This example was more reasonably priced at $5.75.

In the early 1920s, genuine leather underarm bags became the popular mode. Originally called *pochettes* around 1915, this bag was made similar to the earlier pocketbooks designed like an envelope with a flap but now they were designed with a popular top or back strap handle. Many leather varieties were made with the delicate hand tooling further accented with gold leaf. Other examples were enriched with embroidery or embossing which was referred to as "tooled effects." They were continually advertised through the decade as "popular, serviceable, practical and modernistic." Silk varieties were also extremely fashionable in addition to those made of patent leather and leatherette. The underarm style was often made with a gold-colored tinsel tapestry interwoven in a dark-colored background creating a very modern looking bag. Abstract and geometric designs began to surface in addition to Egyptian, African and Mexican motifs characteristic of what would later be known as "Art Deco.".

See additional advertisements for early twentieth century handbags on pages 164 to 172.

Fall fashions from Bergdorf Goodman, circa 1918.

Pin seal evening bag with sterling silver frame. This bag sold for $39.00 in 1918.

Brocaded velvet evening bag with antique sterling silver frame. This bag sold for $68.00 in 1918. *Harper's Bazaar.*

Autumn fashion for October 1917 as
featured in *McCall's*.

Chapter IV:

❊ Beaded Bags

Handmade beaded bags have been fashionable for over two hundred years. Today these wonderful treasures are considered works of art and have become collectible. They are cherished for their beauty as well as their exceptional workmanship. The time and effort spent in constructing beaded handbags is, for many, incomprehensible. Decades ago, some of these bags warranted high prices. For example, around 1800, the standard price for having a knitted bead bag made was a costly $5.00. By the early twentieth century, certain companies in America were offering European beaded bags of the crochet-type for $100.00, an extravagant sum to pay at that time. And so this type of handbag, whether knitted or crocheted, was never an inexpensive accessory. Today these bags are still fetching high prices.

Although these bags can be difficult to date, there are a few indications that can aid in approximating their age. Beaded bags from the middle of the nineteenth century were almost always made with very small, fine beads; up to 1000 beads per square inch can be found on bags dating before 1850. With

Nineteenth century beaded reticule with colorful floral pattern, bottom tassel and drawstring closure.

Beaded bag, deer design, attached to gilded frame with chain handle, nineteenth century.

Beaded reticule fashioned with very fine beads in floral pattern. The drawstring is laced through small crocheted rings and the inside is lined with fine silk cloth, early nineteenth century.

beads this fine, the bag appears cloth-like with movement and complex designs resembling tapestry. Certain bead colors were also unique to earlier periods such as cornflower blue and brick red. In the second half of the nineteenth century, the beads became slightly larger. Somber and sometimes morbid funeral scenes were common in the early 1800s. Then, during the period from 1820 until 1860, wonderful scenes, historic places, pastoral settings, romantic figurals, flora and fauna were popular motifs rendered in beads.

Early beaded bags usually were made in the drawstring style called the reticule. A few distinct characteristics of these early beaded reticules will also help in determining their age. For instance, bags made in the early 1800s were constructed with three definite horizontal sections of beading. The bottom section of the reticule was often beaded in a star pattern with a tassel which was suspended directly from its center point; this was especially common if the bag had a rounded bottom. Bags made with squared bottoms sometimes had fringe instead of a tassel. The middle section of the reticule, which was usually the largest of the three, consisted of a floral or scenic motif. The third section, located at the top of the reticule, was either a scalloped border, a floral border, a sawtooth edge or some other pattern which complimented the overall design. Although there may be exceptions, the basic construction of early beaded reticules were knitted in this manner. The knitted body of the bag was attached to a silk section known as a "header." Ribbon, cord and occasionally chain was drawn through small rings which became the closure and handles of the reticule.

Beaded reticule made with very fine beads, figural motif, silk lining with beaded fringe and drawstring closure.

Two Nineteenth Century beaded reticules.

Small beaded reticule, star pattern at bottom, cornucopia center theme and sawtooth edge, early nineteenth century.

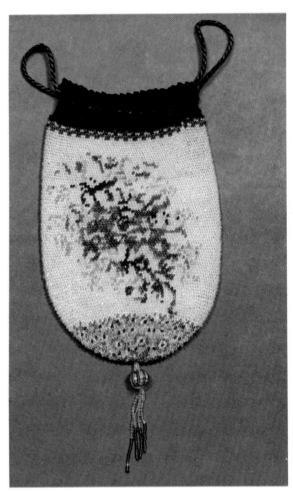

Beaded reticule with dark green crocheted header and cord drawstrings.

Early beaded reticule with three horizontal sections, crocheted silk header and cord drawstring.

In the early 1800s, beaded bags began to be framed with pinchbeck, gold and silver. Less expensive metals, such as brass and copper also were used and embellished with enamel, filigree ornamentation and paste stones. Elaborate frames of this type were usually made in France and Austria. Framed bags of the 1820s and 1830s were frequently made to resemble a pie cut in wedges (up to one dozen wedges) with the separate sections being carefully knitted together. Brightly-colored floral patterns were popular and these bags were usually fringed from one end of the frame to the other.

By the early twentieth century, beaded bags became increasingly fashionable so older beaded bags were taken out of hiding, restored and sometimes reframed for a more up-to-date look. Ornate frames made of solid gold, sterling silver, German silver, nickel, tortoiseshell, amber, ivory, ormolu and celluloid were utilized. Metal frames were heavily engraved, embossed or further accented with gemstones, filigree ornamentation and enamel work. Ivory frames were carved and celluloid frames were molded and sometimes hand-painted. Nineteenth century pattern books also began to resurface and new bags were constructed from old patterns.

Glass beaded bag with plain sterling silver frame and chain handle, English hallmarks, nineteenth century.

In the early 1800s, the patterns that were used for making beaded bags were so cherished that they were only given to select members of the family and passed down for posterity. An interesting tale was told in the book *Two Centuries of Costume* by Alice Morse Earle dealing with "domestic jealously and social envy" concerning the secrecy of the beaded bag patterns:

"In one New England town Matilda Emerson reigned a queen of bagmakers; her patterns were beyond compare; one of a Dutch scene with a windmill was the envy of all who beheld it. She was a rival with Ann Green for the affections of a minister, a solemn widower, whose sister kept house for him and his three motherless children. Matilda gave to the parson's sister the written rules for a wonderful bead bag (the design having originated in Boston), a bag which displayed when finished a funeral willow tree and urn and grass-grown grave, in shaded grays and purple and white on a black ground; a properly solemn bag. But when the pastor's sister essayed to knit this trapping of woe, it proved a sad jumble of unmeaning lines, for Ann Green had taken secretly the rules from the knitter's work-box, and had changed the pencilled rules in every line. When the hodgepodge appeared where orderly symbols of gloom should have been seen, the sister believed that Matilda had purposely written them wrong in order to preserve her prestige as a bag-knitter; and she so prejudiced her brother that he coldly turned from Matilda and married, not Ann, but a widow from another town. Disappointed of her desired husband, Ann tormented herself with her New England conscience until she revealed her wickedness to poor Matilda, whose reinstatement in the parson's esteem could not repay her loss of his affections."

Indeed, these bag patterns were cherished and given only to a select few as neatly guarded secrets.

Shaggy beaded bag attached to oval floral celluloid frame and celluloid link chain. The inside lid has small round mirror and the lid is marked Pat'd. Ap. 25, 1922.

Large framed beaded bag with silhouette motif, early twentieth century.

Beaded bag fashioned with tiny colored glass beads in figural design with engraved silver-plated frame, imitation sapphires set in knob clasps, cloth lined, marked Made In Germany.

Nineteenth century beaded reticule.

Knitted bead purse made with deep red colored beads in swag design with nickel-plated frame, chain handle and chamois lining, circa 1910-1915.

Unusual-shaped carnival glass bugle beaded bag in shaggy bead design, with ornate ormolu frame, filigree ornamentation and bezel-set blue glass stones, beaded handle and changeable silk lining.

Beaded bags are difficult to date because new bags often were made with much older beads. Beads from the early 1800s were sometimes used on bags made in new styles in the 1920s. Also, bags in the 1920s were made with new beads from a century-old pattern. Frames can sometimes provide an indication of the bag's age, but they are not fool-proof either. A beaded bag that is signed and dated by its maker can be reliable proof but, of course, this is a rarity.

Certain identifiable characteristics can help to approximate the dates of particular examples. Beaded bags made with three sections can almost always be dated to the early nineteenth century and circular pie crust bags made with fine beads and floral patterns. Beaded bags with geometric patterns or abstract designs, attached to celluloid frames, date from the early twentieth century. Swag or shaggy bead designs were popular in the second decade of the twentieth century and usually were made in the drawstring reticule or wrist strap style. Beaded bags employing somewhat larger glass beads on a net ground were common in the 1920s and most of the bags were made in Czechoslovakia and Germany with wonderful Bohemian and Bavarian glass beads. Bags with free-flowing lines either in the beadwork or on the frame can be attributed to the Art Nouveau period (1890-1910). Finer beads in complex scenics, florals, figurals or funeral designs indicate an early 1800s vintage. Themes such as peacocks, silhouettes, Egypt and the Orient were popular in the early twentieth century.

Beaded wrist bag done in red silk with French jet beads, shaggy bead fringe and long tassel.

Shaggy bead wrist bag with snap closure and silk lining.

Beaded reticule fashioned with Bohemian glass on black net background, lined with silk, early twentieth century.

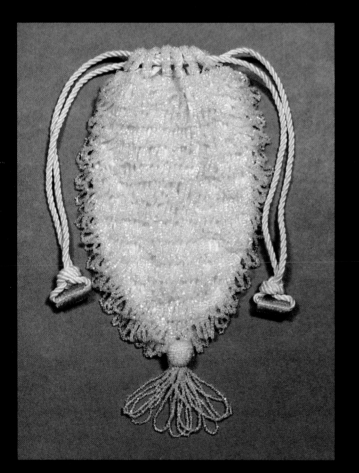

Shaggy beaded reticule with cord drawstring and beaded ball and tassel at bottom. The inside is fitted with coin purse and mirror.

Beaded reticule on net background with design and fringe ending in Van Dyke points, cord drawstrings with bead ornaments on ends, purple silk lining, Made in Czechoslovakia.

Beaded bag with black plastic frame set with rhinestones, silk lining and cord handles.

Left—Beaded bag knitted with carnival glass beads, swag design with nickel-plated frame and chain handle. Top Right—Shaggy beaded wrist bag made with three rows of carnival glass beaded fringe. Bottom Right—Small floral beaded bag with beaded handle, fitted with small round mirror.

Beaded bag, floral pattern with embossed nickel-plated frame and chain handle.

Round beaded wrist bag made of Bohemian glass beads on a net ground.

The island of Murano, which is located about three miles off the coast of Venice, Italy, has been noted for centuries for its wonderful glass industry. Dating back to 1291, glass furnaces were moved to Murano from Venice. From that time Murano has been the chief center for the manufacture of tiny glass beads suitable for professional and amateur bagmakers.

In the sixteenth century, glass furnaces were set up in Bohemia and that small area became noted for wonderful glass beads as well. On a smaller scale, other mountain areas of Germany and Austria also produced glass beads which were used for creating the ultimate in fancy work.

Beads vary in size as well as color. Dozens of colors and different shades of the same color were produced and utilized to create these exceptional bags. Beads were transparent, opaque or iridescent resembling carnival glass. The shapes of the beads also varied from round to elongated bugle beads. The beads used for the body of the bag were usually smaller than those used for making the beaded fringe. Since it has already been established that thinner purse silk was used for the fringe, it is no wonder that the extra weight of the beads on the finer silk caused the fringe to unravel in time. If a finer silk was not available for the fringe, larger beads were used with regular purse silk.

Unusual shaped beaded bag done on heavy stiff canvas with peacock motif, silk lining and fringe in need of repair.

Suede *pochettes* accented with steel beadwork advertised for sale in 1930.

Drawstring reticule fashioned with colored glass beads on a net ground.

Bright colored beaded bag with ornate oxidized metal frame, damask interior, Made in Czechoslovakia.

Beaded bag on net ground with imitation tortoiseshell frame and beaded handle, possibly Czechoslovakia.

Beautiful woven colored cut steel handbag with jeweled frame, satin lining fitted with coin purse, mirror and comb, marked Made in France.

Multi-colored French cut steel handbag with jeweled ornament and push button knob clasp.

Besides requiring the beads to be the perfect size, shape and color, avid bagmakers, especially in New England, raised their own silkworms to produce perfect purse silk. Making a beaded bag was truly a labor of love and the cherished product was passed down from generation to generation.

In the 1820s and 1830s, metal beads and sequins made of brass and steel were used as decorative renderings on accessories such as reticules. By the 1840s, smaller steel beads which were round, square, oblong and even faceted completely covered hand-loomed purses in France. The cut steel beads were chemically dyed in predominantly three shades: silver, gold and bronze. On rare occasions, however, a French cut steel bag will be found in other colors such as pink, purple, green, yellow, blue, black or white creating magnificent floral, oriental or abstract patterns. These rare bags are highly collectible, especially when found with ornate jeweled frames.

The frames of cut steel bags were usually made of gilded base metals, German silver, aluminum, silver or nickel plate with embossed decorations. Elaborate bags warranted elaborate frames and some can be found rendered in precious metals, filigreed, enameled or studded with gemstones. The French cut steel bags also have extraordinary fringe complimenting the magnificent bodies.

Woven cut steel beaded bag studded with imitation sapphire stones, mounted on gilded brass frame with jeweled ornament and push button clasp. The inside of the bag is lined with a changeable silk.

French cut steel bag with nickel-plated frame and double chain handle. The inside of the bag contains a separate frame with attached kid-lined coin purse. *Christine Ketchel.*

French cut steel bag with celluloid frame and link chain.

French cut steel bags were not common in America until the first decade of the twentieth century. After World War I, they were seen in America in abundance and available through mail order catalogues and department stores. American manufacturers also produced cut steel bags but the quality of the steel beads was inferior to that of the French cut steel; American cut steel rusted when it came in contact with moisture or water. For some reason, French cut steel beads did not have this problem. American cut steel beads were also slightly larger but somewhat duller than the French examples. Most of the American cut steel beads were applied to popular round chatelaine bags that were commercially made or used for embellishments on crocheted bags constructed at home. Imported French cut steel beads also were used for the homemade versions.

The exquisite French cut steel bags usually contained fine silk linings and a cloth label that read **France** or **Made in France**. To a lesser degree, Germany and Austria also produced cut steel bags. Aluminum beads were used occasionally in America but these bags are rare. French jet beads (actually black glass) were silvered to resemble genuine cut steel. A much lower price tag accompanied this type of bag.

Crocheted steel beaded bag with large oval-shaped nickel-plated frame, embossed with floral designs and attached to mesh wrist strap handle with slide.

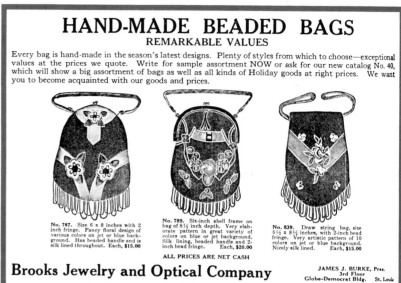

Beaded bags offered for sale in 1919.

Top—American-made cut steel bag with beaded handle and button fastener. Bottom—French cut steel bag, geometric pattern fashioned from three shades of chemically dyed steel beads, attached to gilded copper frame and chain handle.

Lattice-type beadwork (diagonal weaving) with black silk background showing through the beaded network, mounted on steel frame ornamented with cut steel, marked Made in France.

Beautiful colored glass beaded bags from France, Germany, Czechoslovakia and Italy were offered for sale by leading jewelry manufacturers from the turn of the century until the middle of the 1930s. These were exquisite in both quality of materials and workmanship in executing the designs. Besides the typical jewelry companies, other firms distributed these little treasures especially after World War I into the flamboyant flapper era.

The Brooks Optical Company of St. Louis, Missouri, offered handmade beaded bags in 1919. A 6 x 8-inch bag with a two-inch fringe, beaded handle and silk lining retailed for $15.00. Another beaded bag with a six-inch tortoiseshell frame sold for $20.00, while another style made like a drawstring reticule with a two-inch beaded fringe, silk lining and a "very artistic pattern of ten colors on jet or blue background" sold for $15.00.

In 1919, the M. Bonn Company, of Pittsburgh and St. Louis, offered *Bonn Wear* Beaded Bags which ranged in price from $10.50 to $37.00. The bags were somewhat circular or pouch-shaped with knob clasps, beaded handles and fringe. They were available in a variety of patterns and color combinations with changeable and flowered silk linings. Their ad in the *Keystone Magazine* stated that:

"Fancy beaded bags are in style for this Christmas season. Everybody seems to be wanting them and already many wholesalers have exhausted their stocks. However, we have been extremely fortunate in securing a wonderful assortment of these handsome bags in many novel effects and we strongly urge you not to delay sending us your requests, because they are selling like wild-fire."

The ad did not state where they bags originated from but the style was very similar to Czechoslovakian examples.

French cut steel beaded bags featured in the Jason Weiler and Sons Catalogue, circa 1927.

Suede drawstring reticule enriched with beaded fringe.

In 1920, the John V. Farwell Company offered a wonderful selection of imported beaded bags direct from Paris. This Chicago-based firm sold glass beaded bags from $33.00 to $100.00 each. The lowest priced bag was a reticule-style made of blue, grey, green or brown glass beads in assorted patterns with silk linings. Ironically, this 1920s bag was made with the three horizontal sections reminiscent of the earlier nineteenth century vintage but the beads were larger and the pattern not as intricate as examples from the previous century. The header on this bag was constructed with beads whereas a slightly more expensive example was made with a silk header and a beaded handle. A $50.00 bag was made of blue or jet beads with a pattern in silver beads, a silk lining and a tortoiseshell frame. A $75.00 bag had a background of blue beads with the pattern in various colors, silk-lining, and a shell or amber frame. Their most expensive bag, ($100.00), was a combination of blue, green, red, jet and gold beads with a silk lining and an ivory frame. Steel beaded bags from Paris were also offered from $27.00 to $90.00 each. They were made in the reticule style with a drawstring handle which was also made of cut steel beads. Not one of the bags offered from this company in 1920 was constructed with a metal frame.

In 1927, the Jason Weiler & Sons Company offered beaded bags from their Paris office ranging in price from $5.00 to $45.00 each. A $5.00 bag was made of colored glass beads, black jet beads or silvered beads with a silvered finished frame, silk lining, change purse and mirror. A $30.00 colored cut steel bag in a

Transfer patterns for making American Indian designs on beaded bags, McCall's Transfer Patterns, circa 1917.

Indian-style beaded reticule.

Large beaded handbag mounted on Art Nouveau style silver-plated frame with white beaded fringe.

floral pattern and a silvered background was attached to a gold finished frame with an attached chain handle. The larger and most expensive ($45.00) bag was made of the finest cut steel beads that were colored in a floral pattern with a silver-plated gemstone mounted frame, a silk lining with pocket, change purse and mirror. All of the bags from this company had chain handles and fringed bottoms

In the early twentieth century, beaded bags made by American Indians became stylish. These were usually constructed of chamois with bright colored glass beads larger than those used on the traditional beaded bags of the same vintage.[1] Patterns were sold by various companies including McCall's Pattern Agency which enabled women to create this type of bag at home. Transfer patterns of original American Indian designs were sold which could be applied to cloth, silk or chamois using a hot iron. Full beading instructions were also included in the package. Many companies imported beaded bags of different qualities and price ranges. But beaded bags, along with other forms of fancy work, were still constructed by many in their homes. New pattern books were continually being made available with numerous patterns for making these wonderful treasures at home. Step by step instructions were given along with specific information about the size of the beads, the colors and number of bunches necessary to complete the project. Good eyesight, accuracy and patience was needed. A project like this today would warrant a high price, since complex patterns could take up to a year to finish.

---

[1] Beaded bags made by the Iriquois Indians were popular tourist novelties in the nineteenth century.

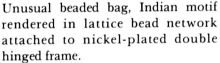

Unusual beaded bag, Indian motif rendered in lattice bead network attached to nickel-plated double hinged frame.

Geometric designs are common on these Czechoslovakian beaded bags made in the 1930s.

In the late 1920s, a new look in beaded bags became fashionable. Envelope-style pouches with back straps and small handbags with beaded or chain handles were made of simulated pearl and pastel beads trimmed with white seed beads and occasionally accented with tambour or Beauvais embroidery. The majority of this type were made in France and Belgium while Czechoslovakia produced similar less expensive versions. The envelope style and small bags with handles were always designed in striking geometrics, lined with ivory-colored grosgrain, and a cloth label attached to an inside pocket that read **Made in Czechoslovakia**. Original bags of this type are abundant on today's market, indicative of their inexpensive original price.

In 1933, H.M.Manheim & Company, of New York City, sold handmade beaded bags from Paris in a wide variety of styles and price ranges. The envelope pouch-style with seed and simulated pearl beads embroidered on white chiffon contained satin linings, inside pockets and double silk-backed mirrors. They retailed for $16.00 each. Other bags from this company were made of cream-colored French seed beads, accented with Beauvais embroidery and black faille bags with black seed beads and hand Beauvais embroidery. The envelope style retailed for $4.50 and the pouch style with chain handle was $11.50. This type of bag remained popular well into the fifties.

Two beaded top-handled bags, geometric designs are zippered closures, marked Made In Czechoslovakia, circa 1930s.

By the 1940s, larger, heavier, box-type bags encrusted with bronze, black, blue, white and even cut steel beads became the height of fashion. Women still enjoyed hand work and this type of handbag became the rage. Commercially-made examples included bags accompanied by a sturdy plastic frame and handle or large braided handles made of beads. A majority of beaded purses of this type were manufactured by DuBonnette, K & G, and the Fre-Mor Company.

See additional advertisements for beaded bags on page 173

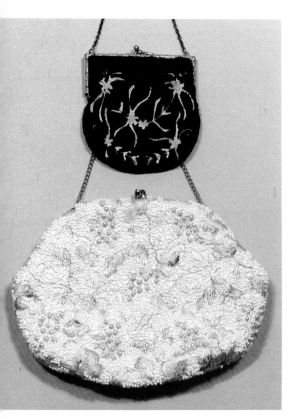

Top—Small black beaded and tambour embroidered evening bag. Bottom—Larger white beaded bag enriched with Beauvais embroidery, marked "Magid", Hand Beaded, Made in U.S.A.

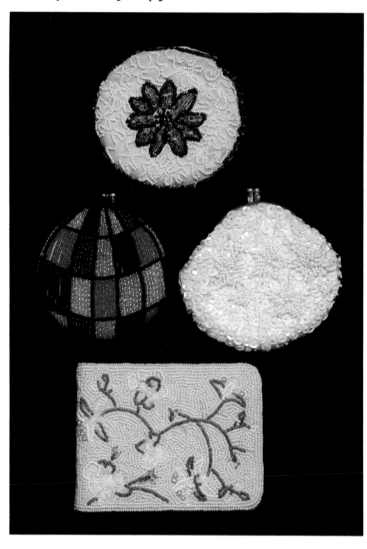

Three beaded coin purses and a wallet made of seed beads accented with Beauvais embroidery.

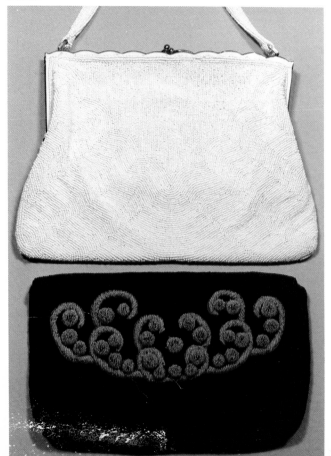

Top—Beaded handbag made of white seed beads with beaded handle and white enameled frame. The inside of the bag is satin lined and marked "Made in Belgium by Hand, Walborg." Bottom—Beaded envelope style underarm bag made of brown and beige beads in raised pattern, marked "Made in Belgium expressly for Sak's Fifth Avenue."

Beaded bags made of simulated pearls and bugle beads offered from Montgomery Ward in 1937.

Bronze beaded bag with plastic frame and lid, heavy braided handle, marked Fre-Mor.

Bronze-colored beaded bag and matching shoes, marked Jasly.

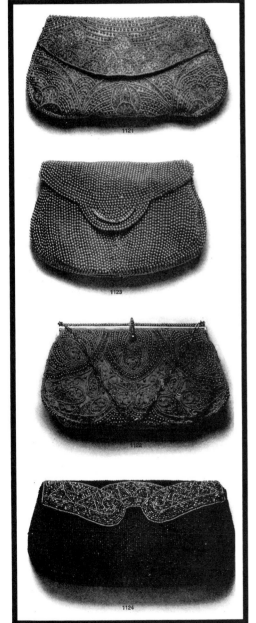

Beaded bags offered for sale in 1933 from the H. M. Manheim Company catalogue.

Bronze beaded bag lined with brown grosgrain, fitted with mirror and lipstick tube.

Beaded hat box bag made of white milk glass beads fashioned in circular patterns, white satin lined, marked "Delill."

Green carnival glass beaded box bag, goldtone frame and clasp, beaded handle, satin lined, two large compartments separated by zippered pockets designed to hold cosmetic cases, marked DuBonnette Original.

Bronze beaded box bag framed in embossed goldtone metal, marked "An Original Fre-Mor Creation."

Black beaded bag framed in silvertone embossed metal, fitted with compartments to hold cosmetic cases, marked "An Original Fre-Mor Creation."

Bronze-colored beaded bag with plastic frame and heavy beaded handle. The inside is lined with satin and is equipped with four inside compartments designed to hold cosmetics.

White beaded wrist pouch with spring tension metal frame covered with beads.

Blue carnival glass beaded box bag with plastic top, metal frame, beaded handle, navy faille lining and large inside mirror.

Cut steel beaded wrist bag with spring-type double hinged frame and brown silk lining, American made.

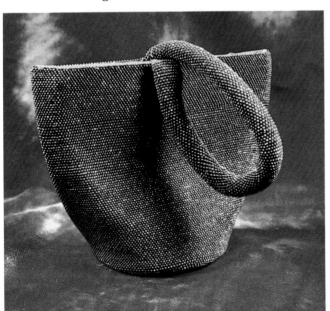

ANOTHER REMARKABLE SALE OF

IMPORTED Bags $5

for Afternoon and Evening

$6.50 to $12.50 Grades

Marvelous values . . . careful shopping compares the finer ones with bags selling elsewhere at higher prices. Beautifully-matched small creamy "pearls"; jet black tubular beads; eggshell or pastel seed pearls, some containing as many as 30,000 beads; soft-colored Beauvais embroideries; lovely Bianchini brocades; metal beads; Persian embroideries; beaded or embroidered silk crepes and satins.

SKETCHED: EIGHT FROM DOZENS OF STYLES—

Bead bag in gilt, silver and black; deeply fringed.

Eggshell seed pearl pouch, Beauvais embroidered; satin-lined.

Beautifully-matched creamy "pearls"; twisted frame of gilt and pearls.

Soft pouch of Bianchini brocade, pale mulberry and gold tones.

Seed pearls and Beauvais embroidery; jade-green stone-set frame.

Dark blue silk pouch, beaded in three shades of blue and steel.

Soft-colored Persian-embroidered envelope; peach-silk-lined.

Black silk crepe envelope, pearl and rhinestone-embroidered; satin-lined.

John Wanamaker's Imported Beaded Bag Sale of December 11, 1930 advertised in a Philadelphia newspaper.

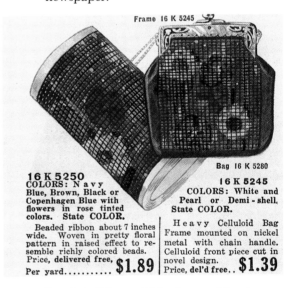

Frame 16 K 5245

Bag 16 K 5280

16 K 5250
COLORS: Navy Blue, Brown, Black or Copenhagen Blue with flowers in rose tinted colors. State COLOR.
Beaded ribbon about 7 inches wide. Woven in pretty floral pattern in raised effect to resemble richly colored beads. Price, delivered free, Per yard......... **$1.89**

16 K 5245
COLORS: White and Pearl or Demi-shell. State COLOR.
Heavy Celluloid Bag Frame mounted on nickel metal with chain handle. Celluloid front piece cut in novel design. Price, del'd free.. **$1.39**

Beaded ribbon sold for bag making in 1920.

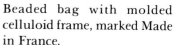

Multi-colored glass beads were used to create this knitted bag with full fringe and floral designs on brass frame.

Opalescent beads were used to create this knitted handbag.

Large beaded reticule, floral motif with crocheted header and drawstring closure.

Large beaded bag, floral motif, hand engraved silver-plated frame, lined in silk with inside pocket.

Beaded bag with ornate metal filigree frame and chain handle. *Christine Ketchel.*

Beaded bag with molded celluloid frame, marked Made in France.

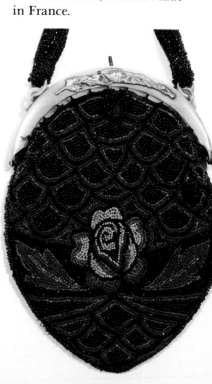

Imported Evening Bags

$6.50 to $12.50
Grades . . . Each $5

Lovely little bags . . . they'll delight any woman, of any age! Simulated pearls in white, black or evening colors; exquisite brocades; chalk beads, gold and silver beads . . at least a dozen fascinating shapes. Each daintily silk or satin-lined, and as charming in every detail as foreign bags always are. Three of many styles are shown:

Mail and Telephone Orders Filled.

Beaded bag with floral designs, knob clasp, cloth lined and beaded handle. *Christine Ketchel.*

Left—Small glass beaded bag with metal frame that was enameled black, cloth lining and ribbon handle. Right—Small steel beaded reticule with beaded ribbon closure and steel beaded fringe. *Christine Ketchel.*

Beaded bags advertised for sale in December of 1930.

Knitted bead bag fashioned with green silk purse twist and clear beads, oxidized frame and chain handle.

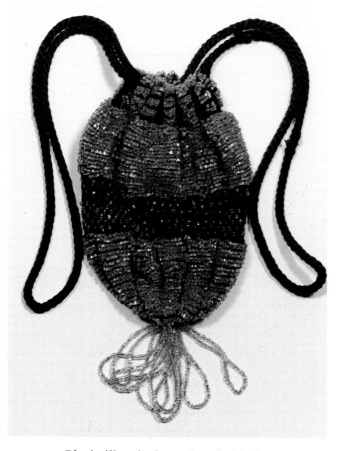

Black silk reticule crocheted with clear glass beads, black cord drawstring and clear glass beaded tassel.

Light blue beaded reticule, diamond pattern, drawstring closure and beaded ball ornaments attached to end of strings.

Two Twentieth Century beaded wrist bags, layered in fringe and lined with silk.

American-made knitted cut steel bag in swag design with ornate silver-plated frame, imitation sapphires set in knob clasp.

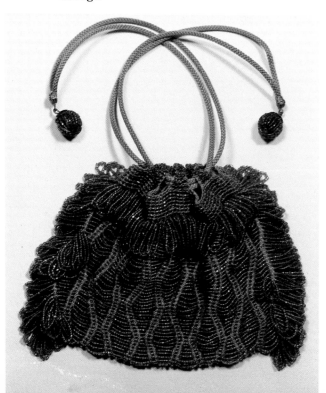

Two Twentieth Century beaded reticules with drawstring closures.

Two Twentieth Century beaded wrist bags, layered in fringe and lined with silk.

Top—Nineteenth century beaded watch pocket. Bottom—Indian beaded purse with large beads fashioned on felt background.

Black and silver beaded bag with beaded fringe, attached to oxidized cathedral dome-shaped frame and attached ribbon handle.

Navy blue grosgrain underarm pouch accented with cut steel beads, marked Made in France.

Large beaded bag, floral design with nickel-plated frame and silk lining.

Beaded evening bag using white and pearl colored beads on a gauze fabric fastened by means of a tambour hook.

Oval zippered beaded back strap pouch and envelope style zippered back strap pouch, marked Hand Made in Belgium.

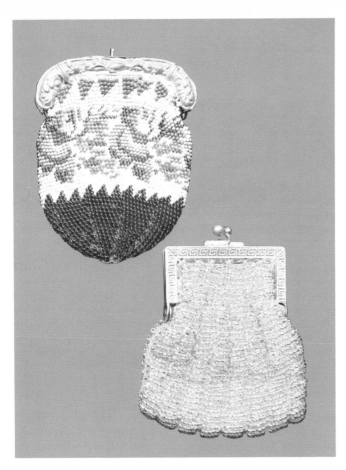

Top—Nineteenth century beaded coin purse. Bottom—Twentieth century beaded coin purse.

Black beaded fashion accessories.

Beaded bag, Made in Hong Kong.

Beaded bag, Hand Made in France.

French beaded handbag with tiny seed beads in floral and paisley patterns, lift lock closure, snake chain handle, silk lined, marked "Fabienne, Paris, 208 Rue De Rivoli."

Beaded bag enriched with tambour work, marked "Hand Made in France for Jorelle Bags." *Christine Ketchel.*

Three beaded clutch bags with zippered tops, marked Made in Japan, circa 1950s.

Two envelope-style beaded clutch bags, circa 1950s.

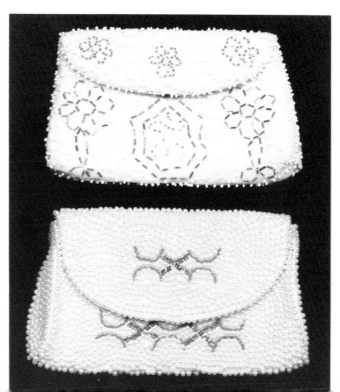

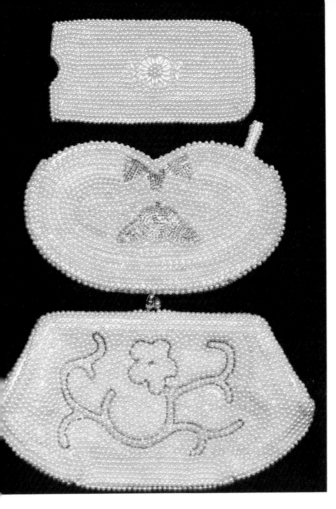

Beaded back strap pouch, marked Hand Made in Belgium.

Eyeglass case and beaded clutch bags Made In Japan.

Two beaded clutch bags, marked "Regal Products, Made in Japan."

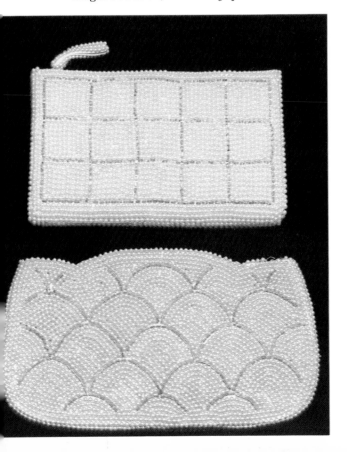

Spring and Summer handbags popular in 1955, Sears.

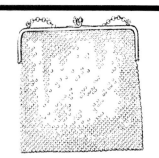

Tapestry *pochette* with flowers outlined in carnival glass beads, inside label reads: "Made in Belgium for Strawbridge and Clothier, Philadelphia."

Black cloth handbag enriched with rosettes of French Jet beads, marked "Soure' Bag, New York."

Imitation pearl evening bags advertised for sale in December of 1930 from John Wanamaker in Philadelphia.

Bright red beaded bag with beaded handle, knob claps, lined with red satin, marked "Bags by Josef and Beaded in France."

8707J2025—**Black Beaded Bag.** A fine imported hand beaded bag with Golden colored snake chain handle. Satin lined and has mirror in compartment. A treasured gift.

Sugg. Retail $30.00

8676J945—**Clutch Bag.** An exquisite finest imported envelope type clutch bag of shimmering Silver crystal beads. The perfect clutch bag for cocktail parties, dinner, theatre, etc.

Sugg. Retail $14.00

8774J3240—**Beaded Bag.** The ultimate in fine beaded bags. Beautiful Black beaded bag with fine beaded handle and delicate Petit-Point frame closure. Matching Black satin lining with inside pocket and mirror.

Sugg. Retail $45.00

Beaded bags offered for sale in the
Bennett Blue Book, circa 1966.

Bronze beaded hat box bag, silk lined
with three inside pockets.

Bronze-colored beaded handbag,
marked "K & G Charlet Bag, Paris,
New York."

Beaded handbag made of black beads
and multi-colored braid in scrolling
designs.

Powder blue beaded handbag, marked Made in Japan.

Commercially-made bronze-colored beaded bag with large twisted bead handle, mirror on inside lid, marked "K & G Charlet Bag, Paris, New York."

Handmade black beaded bag with two layers of fringe on lid.

Left—Black beaded bag, marked "Walborg, Hand Made in Japan." Right—Black beaded bag, marked "Richere, Hand Made in Japan."

Top handled sequined pouch, marked Hand Made in Belgium.

Basket-type bag made of large plastic beads and silver metallic thread, satin lined with inside center coin purse, marked "Made in Italy for Rosenfeld."

Pink beaded wrist bag made of silk and glass beads, chromium frame, watered silk lining, marked "Guaranteed Hand Made."

Hat box beaded bag made of green carnival glass beads, large mirror set in lid, and lined with black silk.

Bronze beaded bag with beaded handle and Mother of Pearl frame and beaded lift lock closure. The inside is lined with satin and label reads: ''Beaded Sweaters and Handbags, Made in Hong Kong.''

Unusual clear plastic handbag covered in ecru lace further accented with white seed beads.

Rhinestone evening bag with top handle and zippered closure, marked Made In Czechoslovakia.

Light blue beaded clutch bag with knob clasp, marked ''Made in Belgium by Hand, Walborg.'' Three round beaded coin purses with zippered closures. The back of each small purse is equipped with round mirror, marked ''Delill, Hand Made in Japan.''

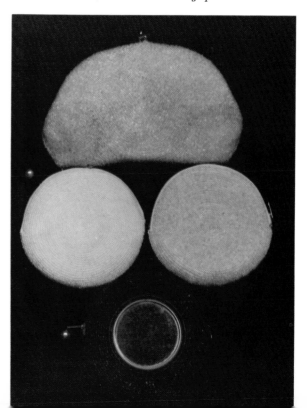

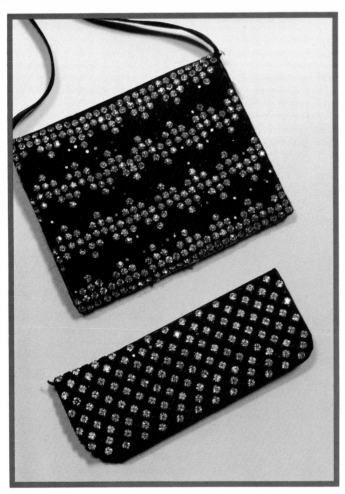

Evening bag and eyeglass case made of silk and studded with clear and black glass stones.

Small framed pouch and matching wallet made of white seed beads enriched with tambour work, marked Made in Paris.

Envelope style clutch bag and matching collar made of simulated pearls, accented with rhinestones on a ground of heavy silver metallic thread.

Beaded box bag.

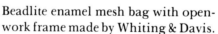

Miniature metal ring mesh bag with double chain handle, marked Made in Germany.

Miniature sterling silver ring mesh purse decorated with seven metal balls suspended from the bottom of the bag. The bag is attached to a chain further ornamented with seven sterling silver charms, English hallmarks found throughout.

Enameled mesh bag, floral design, gilded brass frame, marked Whiting and Davis.

Beadlite enamel mesh bag with open-work frame made by Whiting & Davis.

Ladies' woven wire purse with 50-inch opera chain, spring-hinged lid set with large stone, circa 1899.

Enameled mesh bag with lacquered brass frame, marked Whiting and Davis Company.

Chapter V:

❧ Mesh Bags

As a child, a particular mesh handbag, given to my mother by my grandmother, instinctively remains in the back of my mind. It was kept in a top drawer of my mother's bedroom dresser, hidden from sight. Regardless of its location in space, I was more intrigued by its location in time. Every opportunity I had, I would be in that drawer searching for that bag. Once found, I would gently take it out and hold it up to the light shining through the window. It seemed to glisten and sparkle and its fluid-like appearance entranced me. Carefully, I would lift the chain handle and run the cool metal mesh up and down my arm. Until this day, the feeling of that wonderful old family heirloom still intrigues me.

The company responsible for that lasting memory still exists today. The Whiting and Davis Company, located in Plainville, Massachusetts, was founded as a jewelry firm in 1876. Originally, the firm was called Wade, Davis and Company but changes began to occur in 1880 when young Charles A. Whiting joined the firm. Through hard work, extreme dedication and a desire to somehow recreate a medieval art form, this young man, who was hired as an office apprentice would eventually become owner of the company.

By 1890, Charles Whiting became a partner in the firm. Six years later, when the company was struggling to stay afloat, Whiting, along with Edward Davis and the help of outside investors, managed to keep the business going. By 1907, Whiting repaid all previous loans and managed to buy out Davis' share while keeping the name of Whiting and Davis. Descendents of Charles A. Whiting, including a son-in-law, a grandson and others were actively involved with the firm until 1966. After that date, although no longer owned or operated by a family member, Whiting and Davis, retaining its name, became a subsidiary of an Australian Corporation.

Over 100 years later, from its original inception, the Whiting and Davis Company has been responsible for making exceptional mesh handbags in addition to cigarette cases, lighters, cosmetic clutches, key rings, wallets, picture frames, collars, jewelry and extravagant mesh clothing. Shark outfits for divers and protective hand coverings for butchers are manufactured by Whiting and Davis today. A tremendous amount of hand work still goes into the production of their wonderful products.

Handbags made of metal were not totally unheard of in the nineteenth century. Woven metal mesh bags were made as early as the 1820s. These early bags were usually constructed by skilled gold or silversmiths utilizing those precious metals. When steel jewelry and accessories were in vogue, woven mesh bags made of spun steel were highly fashionable. The first ring mesh or chain work bags, made in the fourth quarter of the nineteenth century, were constructed like medieval armor of flexible interlocking metal rings. Again, skilled craftsmen assembled these bags by hand but as popularity escalated, this time consuming process was extended to others outside of the work place. Very patient women, at home in their leisure time, would carefully assemble

Large silver-colored beadlite mesh bag with gatetop frame, cloth lined and label that reads: "Made in US Zone Germany."

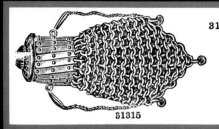

CHAIN PURSES.

31315 Heavy Roman gold fin- doz.
ish, on a steel base, frame
expands 2¼ inches in
diameter, a fine made and
durable chain purse, em-
bossed cover, set with
large stone, setting as-
sorted colors, length of
chain 24 inches.......... 4 00

31315

Chain purses offered for sale in 1899.

Ring mesh purse with finger ring attachment, circa 1895.

Ladies' chain work purse offered for sale in 1895.

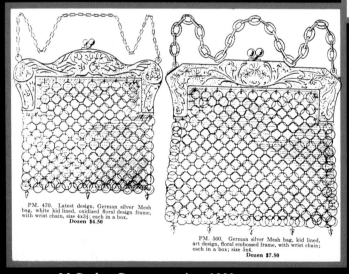

PM. 470. Latest design, German silver Mesh
bag, white kid lined, oxidized floral design frame,
with wrist chain, size 4x3½; each in a box.
Dozen $4.50

PM. 560. German silver Mesh bag, kid lined,
art design, floral embossed frame, with wrist chain;
each in a box; size 5x4.
Dozen $7.50

M.Gerber Company, circa 1900.

METAL PURSES

HERE'S A WINNER.   ABSOLUTELY GUARANTEED THE BIGGEST VALUE IN THE WORLD FOR THE
MONEY.   IN ALL OF OUR BUSINESS EXPERIENCE WE HAVE NEVER GIVEN SUCH
BIG VALUE AT SO LITTLE A PRICE.

No. 1248   German Silver Mesh Bag, size 6½ inches high by 6¼ inches wide, solid German silver frame, fancy embossed and polished, fish scales body, full leather lined, **long chain handle,** ball ends; the biggest value on
the market at our price.   Each... **$2.50**

No. 1246   German Silver and silver plated Mesh bag, size 5¼ inches wide by 5¼ inches deep, as shown in the lower
cut on this page; solid struck one piece German silver frame, fancy embossed, fish scales **mesh, ball ends,**
full leather lined; exceptionally big value at our price.   Each............................... **$1.75**

Metal purses referred to as "fish scale
mesh" offered for sale from Halsman
& Alter, Chicago, Illinois, circa 1898.

German silver ring mesh handbag, kid
lined with inside coin pocket, circa
1900.

the ring mesh by hand. Because of the time necessary to produce this mesh, early handbags, especially those executed in precious metals were very costly. Towards the close of the nineteenth century, however, mesh bags were beginning to be made of less expensive materials which enabled the price to drop considerably. These early mesh bags were made in the chatelaine style, the finger ring style and finally those designed to be hand carried. Most of the early examples assumed rather small proportions.

In 1895, the BHA Illustrated Catalogue advertised Ladies' Purses made of chain work on nickel silver and they were fashioned with decorative chatelaine tops or made with the attached finger ring which was very characteristic of that decade.

In 1899, another mail order company advertised their chain mesh purses accented with heavy Roman gold finishes on a steel base. This type was made with a flexible gatetop frame which expanded 2¼ inches in diameter suspended from a twenty-four inch metal chain.

By 1902, Sears, Roebuck and Company offered metal chatelaine bags "made with fancy links of white metal, silver finish with chain belt hook" for forty-nine cents. Another variation was a design that Sears called a "reproduction of the high priced all silver purse." This example, made of nickel or various other silvered white metals retailed for seventy-five cents.

In 1909, mesh manufacturers were thrilled with the invention of the mesh making machine. A.C.Pratt of Newark, New Jersey was responsible for this invention. With the development of such a modern machine, mesh bags could be mass produced in less expensive materials such as German silver, gunmetal and other white metals and plated with nickel, silver, gold or platinum. Vermeil, which was a gold plating over sterling silver, was also common. Manufacturing this popular accessory now became an easy process. The time now spent in production was minimal and the price was lowered accordingly making this accessory affordable to almost everyone.

By 1912, mesh handbags had become so popular that they were continually advertised as free premiums in fashion and needlework magazines for subscribing to the particular publication that featured them. One publication pictured a meshed coin purse made in the reticule style with a finger ring attached. It was given free with three subscriptions to a newspaper called *Happy Hours*. The ad stated the following:

> "Many novelties soon become necessities and this handy Coin-Purse in solid white metal demonstrates that fact. The size, when opened, is 2½ inches wide and 2½ inches deep. When closed it looks like the picture. It is made of finely meshed rings, with strong chain and large ring to hang on finger. The chain slips through the top rings, and serves to close the opening. Every lady should own one of these dainty little purses. A considerable amount of change may be carried in one of them and is always ready for immediate use. We do not know of anything which will be more popular during this season. For a holiday—or birthday-gift it is a most excellent choice."

Through a considerable amount of research in periodicals from that time period, these ads were extremely common and mesh bags were available almost everywhere.

Mesh bags made of silver gilt were the most common but it was stated in a fashion magazine in 1910 that solid gold bags were "by no means rare and one can pay $25,000. for a jewel studded gold mesh bag, if one has the money and wants to burn it that way." Industrialization created a large wealthy class and the opulent society which existed in the early twentieth century spent a great deal of money on lavish possessions.

German silver ring mesh bags became a ubiquitous accessory from the turn of the century until the early twenties. These bags were made available in all sizes and styles with ornate frames which were either engraved or embossed.

McCall's, circa 1912.

A 1912 advertisement for a free silver mesh handbag.

Mesh bag, silver-plated ornate openwork frame, imitation sapphires set in knob clasps, unmarked.

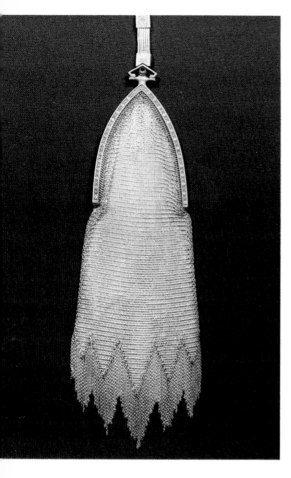

The frames were heavily silver-plated and often lacquered to prevent tarnishing. They displayed characteristics of the free-flowing Arts and Crafts style; flowers, leaves, intertwining vines and scrolling designs were common in the first, second and even the third decade of the twentieth century. The squared bottom of the mesh bag was often decorated with small metal balls or drops and occasionally the mesh was shirred at the frame. Edwardian characteristics, also popular at this time, were created with sophisticated engraving and engine-turned designs. The bags were frequently lined with kid leather and equipped with an inside coin pocket.

A stunning example of a German silver mesh purse was offered from the M. Gerber Company. The chain link mesh, which was shirred at the frame, had additional character because of the chain work rosettes which completely encircled the bag in two different locations. The bottom of the bag ended in Van Dyke or triangular points also made of ring mesh tipped with "additional metal drops." The inside of the bag was lined with kid leather supplemented by an inside coin pocket. The heavily silver-plated and lacquered frame was embossed with an ornate rose design. The bag was attached to an eighteen-inch rope chain. Considering the amount of work involved in making this purse, its turn of the century wholesale price was only $3.90. For an additional dime, a slightly larger frame was available with an amethyst mounted in the center of the frame.

Mesh bags, made in the reticule style, were also popular. M. Gerber offered German silver reticule bags with metal drawstrings. They referred to these particular examples as "Fox-tail Chain Draw Strings." Other sources called this same type of mesh bag a "Dorothy Bag." Different finishes were available for metal mesh bags including French Gray or Platinum, bright or oxidized.

Sterling silver baby fine soldered mesh bag with cathedral dome-shaped frame, sapphires set in knob clasps, mesh strap handle, marked "Whiting and Davis Co. Pat'd. Feb. 1, 1921." *Peg Harnack.*

German silver ring mesh bag with ornate embossed frame, marked "Ger. Sil. Mesh."

German silver ring mesh handbag with embossed frame, marked "R.G. Ger. Silver."

Mesh bag given as free premium for subscribing to *McCall's*, circa 1912.

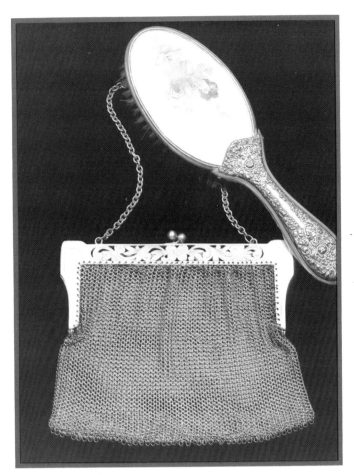

Large German silver ring mesh bag decorated with metal drops and embossed frame, marked "G. Silver."

German silver ring mesh bag with engraved frame, long chain handle and five metal drops suspended from bottom of bag.

German silver ring mesh bag with green gold finish, openwork and engraved frame and chain handle.

German silver shirred ring mesh handbag with Rose design and 18-inch rope chain handle offered for sale in 1900 from the M. Gerber Company.

German silver ring mesh bag with oxidized finished top and 18-inch chain handle featured in the M. Gerber catalogue, circa 1900.

Ring mesh bag made of gunmetal with openwork and hand engraved frame and chain handle. The inside is silk lined with a little metal tag that reads "Real Gunmetal." France.

Gunmetal ring mesh bag with plain gunmetal frame and chain handle, France.

Black enameled mesh handbag.

Enameled mesh bag bearing Whiting and Davis' shield-shaped paper tag.

Two enameled mesh bags with embossed and engraved nickel-plated frames, both unmarked.

The French produced quality handbags made of gunmetal. Although extremely plain, they were very durable. Moreover, like their cut steel beads, gunmetal was rust-proof.

Mesh handbags were the rage for many years and because of their immense popularity, many companies began manufacturing them. A top of the line company like Whiting and Davis, always marked their bags with the company's trademark in miniature, either on the frame or on a metal tag attached to the frame. Some bags included both methods of marking, the stamp in miniature and the metal tag. Occasionally, a shield-shaped paper tag was attached to the bag bearing a description that read "A Whiting and Davis Mesh Bag", with the actual trademark below it. These shield-shaped tags came in two colors: blue for a bag of soldered mesh and white for everything else but soldered mesh. Early examples can also be found with the initials **WD** on the inside of the frame (whether this represented Whiting and Davis or Wade Davis is vague). The words, Whiting and Davis, in very plain lettering, stamped on the inside frame, can also be found on early examples. Many other companies involved in the production of mesh bags did not include such identifiable marks.

Wrist-type mesh bags became the rage in the second decade of the twentieth century. A new baby-fine mesh was made on a new type of mesh making machine. Baby-fine mesh could be made of solid gold, sterling silver or gilded base metals. It was offered either soldered or unsoldered and the price varied accordingly. In 1922, Whiting and Davis offered their "Princess Mary" mesh bag which was made of silver-plated baby-fine soldered mesh. The wholesale price for this particular bag was $42.00. The identical bag in unsoldered mesh was $12.70 indicative of the amount of time spent in manufacturing the soldered versions. This mesh was so fine that it had been said "if spiders were silversmiths they could not weave more scintillant tapestry than the beautiful gold, silver and plated fabrics of which these mesh bags are fashioned." These bags were fringed or decorated with metal drops suspended from the bottom of the bag. Some thin-modeled frame bags had delicate scalloped edges which resembled lace patterns. Seed pearls were also occasionally used for further embellishment. The cathedral dome-shaped frame was extremely popular with baby-fine mesh and a mesh strap handle. Frames were often hand engraved and set with real or imitation sapphires mounted in knob clasps.

Soldered baby fine mesh attached to cathedral dome-shaped frame, marked Whiting and Davis.

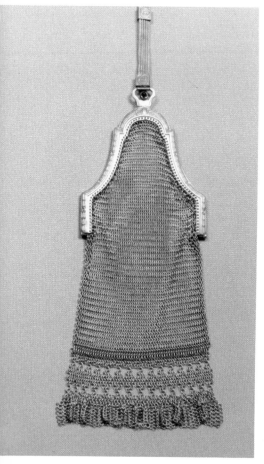

Baby fine mesh bag with green gold finish, mesh strap handle and imitation sapphires set in knob clasps, shirred fringe bottom. *Christine Ketchel.*

Small enameled mesh handbag, unmarked. *Amber Lee Ettinger.*

Silver plated mesh wrist bag with rope chain handle, monogrammed frame and imitation amethysts set in knob clasp, unmarked.

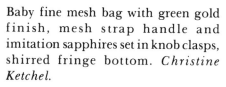

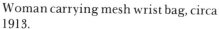

Woman carrying mesh wrist bag, circa 1913.

"Princess Mary" Mesh Bag, *Pictorial Review*, circa November, 1922.

Woman holding fine mesh bag with cathedral dome frame and mesh strap handle, *Vogue*, September, 1918.

Baby-fine mesh went one step further. It became almost material-like when it was enameled in various colors. The designs became like miniature woven tapestries. Soft pastel colors were utilized creating impressionistic designs. These bags, made by Whiting and Davis, were called "Dresden" enamels. Other companies tried to imitate the originals made by Whiting and Davis but no one really came close to the quality of the mesh or the enamel itself.

As the years went on and fashionable women still preferred this type of metal evening bag, new styles and features began to appear to make mesh bags more appealing. For example, vanity boxes were "cleverly concealed in the purses frame." Small powder boxes were designed on the wrist cord. Watches were even mounted right into the frame or on the body of the bag. A mesh bag with the new bracelet frame was popular in the early twenties. Others had complete vanity tops, advertised as "miniature beauty shops with comb, mirror, rouge and powder." Tapestry mesh (black and white enamel) and sunset mesh (red gold-, green gold-, and platinum-finish) made its appearance around 1921-1922.

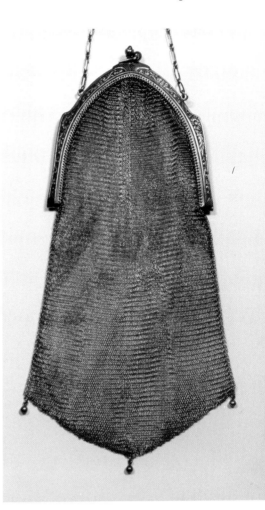

Silver-plated soldered baby fine mesh bag with cathedral dome-style frame and simulated sapphires set in knob clasps, marked Whiting and Davis Company.

Green gold filled baby fine mesh bag with hand engraved frame, sapphire set knob clasp, tassel ornamented with seed pearls and the inside marked Soldered Mesh.

Cathedral dome-shaped frame with enameled mesh bottom and twisted wire chain handle. This bag is marked "Made in Canada."

Dresden enamel mesh bag with enameled frame, unmarked.

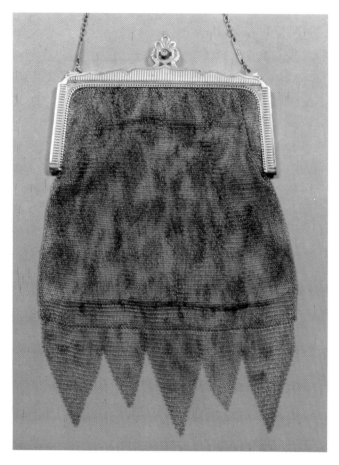

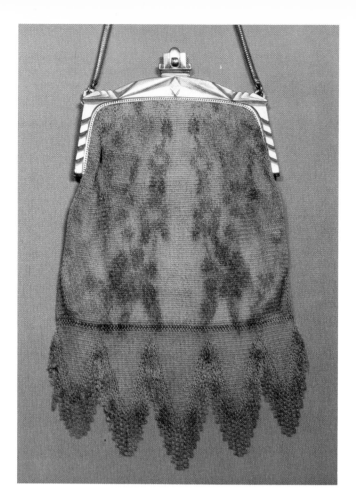

Dresden enamel mesh bag by Whiting and Davis.

Dresden enamel mesh bag mounted on gilded geometric frame, silk lined, inside pocket fitted with small round mirror, marked Whiting and Davis.

Dresden enameled mesh bag, silk lined with modernistic Art Deco silver plated frame, marked Whiting and Davis. *Christine Ketchel.*

Dresden enamel mesh bag with modernistic frame, marked "Soldered mesh by Whiting and Davis."

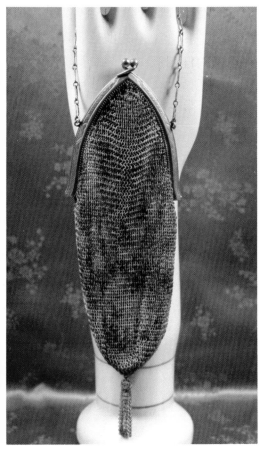

Dresden enamel mesh bag with cathedral dome-shaped frame.

Dresden enamel mesh bag with enamel frame and chain handle, unmarked.

Small mesh bag with round vanity top, nickel plated, unmarked.

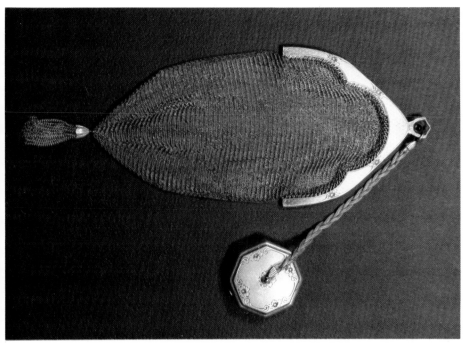

Baby mesh bag with attached compact on mesh strap handle, marked "Sterling soldered mesh, Bliss."

Evans mesh vanity bag with cloisonné compact lid.

Evans mesh vanity bag opened to reveal cosmetic compartments.

Black and white enameled mesh bag by Whiting and Davis.

Black and white enameled mesh bag attached to ornate filigree frame, marked "E L—S A H."

Large enameled flat mesh bag, floral designs, jeweled frame, marked Mandalian Mfg. Co. USA.

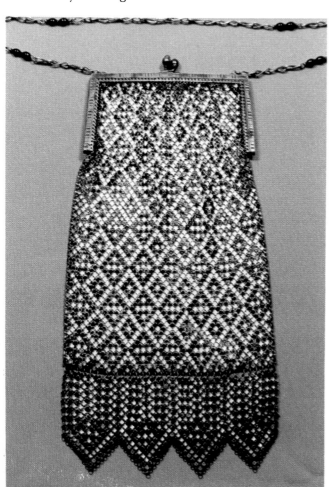

The "Delysia Vanity Bag" made by Whiting and Davis was extremely stylish between 1922 and 1925. This unusual mesh bag resembled a Chinese lantern and was designed to open up in the bag's center-most point which was also its largest area. One side contained rouge and powder compartments while the opposite side had a separate compartment for money or other items. This bag was attached to a metal wrist strap and a tassel of mesh hung from the bottom. It was available in sterling silver, silver plate, green gold plate, nickel silver and tri-colored sunset mesh. It also came either in soldered or unsoldered varieties ranging in price from $10.50 to $60.00.

The "Baby Peggy Mesh Bag" was similar in shape to the Delysia but it was made like a reticule with a metal drawstring, a silk header and a mesh bottom. Both styles of the above mentioned purses were made in baby-fine mesh or flat armor (fish scale) mesh which was enameled.

In the early 1920s, Shatiel Mandalia, a Turkish emigrant began manufacturing enameled mesh bags bearing striking resemblances to those made by Whiting and Davis. Mandalia's firm, known as Mandalian Manufacturing Company was located in North Attleboro, Massachusetts. Mesh handbags bearing the Mandalian trademark were made with a patented "Lustro Pearl Finish." This pearlized enamel, which was guaranteed to be chip resistant, gave a charming glow. The colors were extremely rich and the frames were more ornate that those made by Whiting and Davis. A tremendous amount of filigree and gemstone ornamentation was employed in the frames made by Mandalian. The majority of Mandalian bags were designed with a V-shaped bottom and very fine metal fringe as compared to the many squared bottom bags made by Whiting and Davis.

Although Mandalia opened his factory in 1898 and manufactured silver-plated bags along with other jewelry items, it was his armor mesh enameled creations of the twenties and thirties that gained him his notoriety. By the late twenties, these popular enameled bags were advertised in trade journals and leading jewelry catalogues. The bags were offered in a large spectrum of colors and fabulous designs which included florals, geometrics and oriental designs. They were available with or without an inside lining and the frames were oxidized with extra enamel ornamentation. Prices ranged from $4.00 to $30.00 each in 1929.

Beautiful enameled mesh bag with ornate embossed frame, metal fringe, chain handle, silk lining, marked Mandalian Mfg. Co.

Enameled mesh bag with embossed frame, marked Mandalian Mfg. Co. USA.

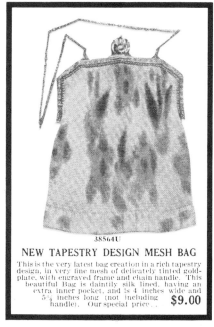

38564U

NEW TAPESTRY DESIGN MESH BAG

This is the very latest bag creation in a rich tapestry design, in very fine mesh of delicately tinted gold-plate, with engraved frame and chain handle. This beautiful Bag is daintily silk lined, having an extra inner pocket, and is 4 inches wide and 5½ inches long (not including handle). Our special price.. **$9.00**

Jason Weiler and Sons, circa 1927.

Child's Mesh Bag 26T1511— Make your little girl happy with this Children's Mesh Bag of Silver plated metal. It is made of fine links with a silver plated metal frame and chain. About 3 inches long. Good quality and a big value. **69¢** Postage 3¢ extra.

Silver-plated child's mesh handbag offered from the National Cloak and Suit Company in 1925.

No. 301   **$15.00 each**

Oxidized top, silk lined, lustro pearl,
medium fine, 4 x 8 inches

No. 300   **$30.00 each**

Enameled top, silk lined, lustro pearl,
baby mesh, 4½ x 9 inches

No. 302   **$24.00 each**

Oxidized top, silk lined, lustro pearl,
medium fine, 4½ x 8¾ inches

No. 304   **$18.00 each**

Oxidized top, silk lined, lustro pearl,
XX grade, 4½ x 8½ inches

No. 305   **$15.00 each**

Oxidized top, silk lined, lustro pearl,
XX grade, 4½ x 8 inches

No. 303   **$15.00 each**

Oxidized top, silk lined, lustro pearl,
XX grade, 4½ x 8½ inches

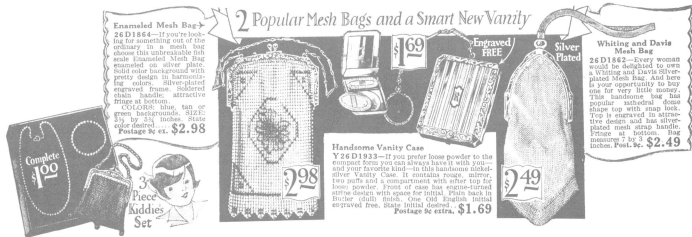

2 Popular Mesh Bags and a Smart New Vanity

Enameled Mesh Bag→
26 D 1864—If you're looking for something out of the ordinary in a mesh bag choose this unbreakable fish scale Enameled Mesh Bag enameled on silver plate. Solid color background with pretty design in harmonizing colors. Silver-plated engraved frame. Soldered chain handle; attractive fringe at bottom.
COLORS: blue, tan or green backgrounds. SIZE: 3½ by 5¾ inches. State color desired..... **$2.98**
Postage 9¢ ex.

$1.69 Engraved FREE Silver Plated

Whiting and Davis Mesh Bag
26 D 1862—Every woman would be delighted to own a Whiting and Davis Silver-plated Mesh Bag. And here is your opportunity to buy one for very little money. This handsome bag has popular cathedral dome shape top with snap lock. Top is engraved in attractive design and has silver-plated mesh strap handle. Fringe at bottom. Bag measures 7 by 3 inches. Post. 9¢. **$2.49**

$2.98

Handsome Vanity Case
Y 26 D 1933—If you prefer loose powder to the compact form you can always have it with you—and your favorite kind—in this handsome nickel-silver Vanity Case. It contains rouge, mirror, two puffs and a compartment with sifter top for loose powder. Front of case has engine-turned stripe design with space for initial. Plain back in Butler (dull) finish. One Old English initial engraved free. State initial desired.. **$1.69**
Postage 9¢ extra.

$2 49

Complete $1.00

3 Piece Kiddies Set

Little Girls' Gift Set
Necklace, Bracelet and Mesh Bag
26 D 1818—This Set includes a pretty 12-inch necklace of Indestructible Pearl beads, a pearl bead bracelet to match and a silver-plated Mesh Bag. Necklace has metal clasp. Bracelet is coiled on a spring and fits any wrist. The bag has engraved silver color metal top. About 2¾ inches deep.
COLORS: white, rose or tan pearl beads. **$1.00**
State color........................Set.

Mesh bags featured in The National Bellas Hess Company catalogue of 1928.

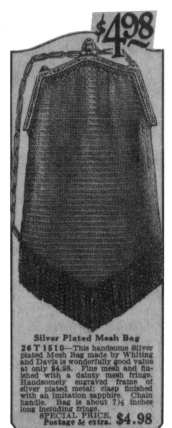

Enameled mesh bag by Mandalian.

$4.98

Silver Plated Mesh Bag
26 T 1510—This handsome Silver plated Mesh Bag made by Whiting and Davis is wonderfully good value at only $4.98. Fine mesh and finished with a dainty mesh fringe. Handsomely engraved frame of silver plated metal; clasp finished with an imitation sapphire. Chain handle. Bag is about 7½ inches long including fringe.
SPECIAL PRICE. **$4.98**
Postage 5¢ extra.

Large enameled mesh bag, oriental design, jeweled and enameled frame, marked Mandalian Mfg. Co. USA.

Opposite page:
Advertisement for enameled mesh handbags made by the Mandalian Manufacturing Company, featured in *The Keystone*, September, 1929.

Fine mesh handbag featured in the National Cloak and Suit Company catalogue of 1925.

"Deauville" mesh bags by Miller Brothers, New York, circa 1922.

Enameled mesh handbag with geometric frame and silk lining, marked Whiting and Davis.

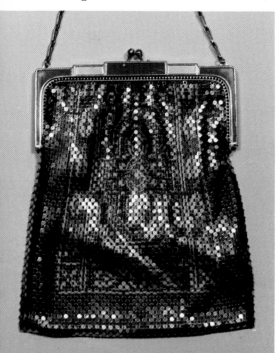

By the early 1940s, the Mandalian Manufacturing Company closed its doors and Whiting and Davis acquired their mesh-making machines. Mandalian mesh handbags were also stamped with the company's trademark on the inside of the purse's frame.

In the late teens and early twenties, Henry Wiener and Son, of New York, advertised their "Picadilly" mesh bags which were "styled with a distinctiveness that distinguishes the usual from the unusual, modish, with the new and patented feature of vanity box containing powder-puff and mirror cleverly concealed in its frame." These bags were constructed of baby fine mesh in 14K gold, sterling silver, silver plate and gold plate with the "latest patterns of very thin model frames."

The immense popularity for mesh handbags prompted imitators. The Automatic Meshbag Company of Providence, Rhode Island manufactured mesh handbags in all shapes and sizes. Advertised as "Gifts that Last", these bags were made of soldered mesh that was soft and silk-like, yet exceptionally strong, appealing to all "fastidious women."

In 1920, John V. Farwell Company, of Chicago, Illinois, offered a wonderful assortment of mesh handbags from $7.25 to $87.50. The least expensive style was made of silver-plated German silver unsoldered baby fine mesh with an oxidized frame and chain handle. A medium priced bag, costing $32.50, was made of soldered German silver but plated with a green-gold finish with an oxidized frame and chain handle. The most expensive model was made of sterling silver with a choice of either a silver finish or a green-gold finish. Their version of the "Picadilly" mesh bag was made of soldered German silver baby fine mesh accented with an 18K green gold finish. It contained a vanity puff and mirror which was concealed in the purse frame and the bottom was V-shaped with three metal drops added at each point for embellishment. This type of bag sold for $52.50 and was advertised as the "most popular bag on the market."

In 1922, Sanderson Manufacturing Company of Providence, Rhode Island promoted their line of unsoldered mesh handbags in new shapes and new trimmings with silver or green-gold finishes to retail for $4.00 and $5.00 each. In the same year, Miller Brothers of New York advertised their mesh bags exclusively known as "Deauville." These bags were also made of baby fine mesh with the envelope type of frame and fold over mesh flap known as the "Princess Mary." Also offered were the cathedral dome framed wrist bags with attached vanity cases.

In 1923, the Ft. Dearborn Watch and Clock Company advertised exquisite sterling silver, gold-and silver-plated soldered baby mesh bags. Over a dozen different shapes were offered including their new bracelet-type frame and handle and the fashionable cathedral dome frame with the mesh strap handle. Conventional shaped bags were also available with etched designs on the frames and sapphire stone-set clasps. Prices ranged from $8.25 for a silver finished bag with a 2½ inch frame that was fully etched and a tassel on the bottom to an expensive $105.00 bag which was made of sterling silver with a 5¼ inch frame set with a sapphire in a knob clasp.

Born out of the Jazz Age, the Roaring Twenties Flapper needed an accessory just as unique and daring as she was. Mesh bags became modernistic, sleek as well as elegant. Deeper, darker colors were utilized on enameled mesh purses. Floral themes were popular in addition to original creations. On one hand, ornate frames were still popular, either gem-mounted, filigreed or enameled, while on the other hand, streamlined designs prevailed. The geometric and abstract motifs, blossoming from this new artistic movement, dominated the designs creating bold and striking patterns and color combinations. Mesh bags now ended in stepped patterns with zig zag designs and fringe. The earlier counterparts were more delicate with lacy and scalloped edges and fine tassels sometimes tipped with seed pearls.

Popularity for these charming and versatile accessories escalated even further when the stars of the silver screen were seen using mesh handbags. In December of 1928, a Christmas advertising campaign for Whiting and Davis mesh bags was featured in the *Ladies' Home Journal*. It was a specific promotion for their Dresden enameled mesh bags and the promoting was done by prominent Hollywood celebrities. The ad stated that:

> "You may not have any stars of the silver screen on your list, but there isn't a woman or girl who won't be simply delighted to have you make this a Whiting and Davis Christmas for her. You'll give her not only a gift of lasting beauty and usefulness, but one that will add a colorful touch of up-to-dateness to her costumes."

Every woman at that time wanted to own a mesh bag for day or evening wear; many wanted one for each outfit. Whiting and Davis made sure that their name became a household word. They advertised their bags more than any other company and obviously, it paid off. This company is still producing fine mesh handbags today.

A stunning geometric design is rendered in enamel in this mesh bag by Whiting and Davis.

Enameled mesh bag with nickel-plated geometric frame, marked Whiting and Davis Company.

Small mesh bag made of armor mesh, embossed frame and metal balls suspended from bottom and sides of bag.

Miniature Dresden-style enameled mesh bag with gilded brass frame and chain handle, unmarked.

Opposite page top right:
Two Whiting and Davis mesh shoulder bags from the recent Heritage Collection, circa 1986. The inside label reads: "Whiting and Davis Heritage Collection, 1986, 110th Anniversary."

Opposite page bottom right:
Whiting and Davis mesh shoulder bag from the 1986 Heritage Collection.

Whiting and Davis mesh bags advertised as graduation gifts in June, 1930.

In 1926, Whiting and Davis celebrated their Golden Anniversary. In 1976, their centennial celebration took place with the production of a limited edition of sterling silver mesh bags. The Star series from the Heritage Collection was another limited edition of mesh bags enameled with faces of prominent Hollywood stars. Four different bags were included in this series. The most popular was Charlie Chaplin, which was rendered in black and white enamel; Clark Gable done in colored enamel; Marion Davies, also done in colored enamel; and finally Renee' Adoree'. Sadly, these bags were not as popular as Whiting and Davis anticipated; few were sold and, as a result, they are extremely rare today. In 1986, another facet of the Heritage Collection, Whiting and Davis manufactured "a limited group of retrospective handbags reminiscent of days gone by." A charming little card was attached to each bag announcing this special celebration and it stated that the bags were "Exclusively designed to capture the charm of yesterday." Although they were quite charming, there is no comparison with the mesh bags that were made decades earlier.

In 1929, French couturier Paul Poiret created a new line of pouch-shaped mesh bags for Whiting and Davis, either in soldered mesh or beadlite enamel. Prices ranged from $13.50 for an "Enameled Petite Armor" mesh bag with Poiret's inspiration "lipstick frame" to $75.00 for a sterling silver soldered mesh pouch-style bag with a silk lining and hand-engraved frame.

Elsa Schiaparelli, Italian-born French fashion designer also began designing a new line of mesh bags for Whiting and Davis. Unlike the traditional bags of the period, they were larger in size and unusual in shape. Armor mesh was employed as well as facet-mesh and beadlite enamel. These bags were fashionable in the late 1930s.

In 1936, Schiaparelli created a stunning "Vanity Box" bag made of gold-colored armor mesh with a mesh ribbon handle. Inside, a silk lining included a large mirror and shirred pocket. In 1937, *Harper's Bazaar* commented:

"There is the typical Schiaparelli touch in the way these new bag designs of hers combine Parisian chic with French practicality. Each of them is so different from the other and yet so perfectly apropos for its own special time and place."

In this same period, larger mesh was beginning to be used for bags designed for day wear. Large bags, made in the pouch style, sometimes had a heavy celluloid frame and handle, or had no frame but a zippered closure. The bags had a cloth label inside displaying the Whiting and Davis trademark. Smaller back strap pouches were fashioned in shell mesh, baguette mesh and armor mesh.

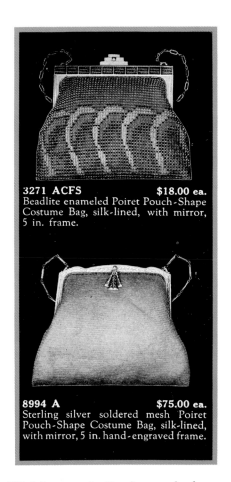

3271 ACFS   **$18.00 ea.**
Beadlite enameled Poiret Pouch-Shape Costume Bag, silk-lined, with mirror, 5 in. frame.

8994 A   **$75.00 ea.**
Sterling silver soldered mesh Poiret Pouch-Shape Costume Bag, silk-lined, with mirror, 5 in. hand-engraved frame.

Whiting and Davis mesh bags "Inspired by the personal designs of Paul Poiret." *The Keystone,* September, 1929.

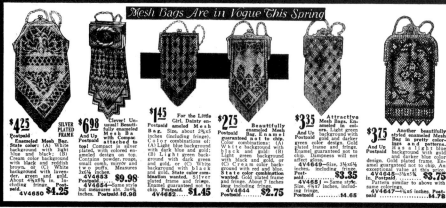

Mesh bags featured in the Sears catalogue of 1930.

Whiting and Davis bags designed by Schiaparelli. *Harper's Bazaar*, October, 1937.

"Vanity Box" made of armor mesh, designed by Schiaparelli for Whiting and Davis. *Vogue*, March 1, 1936.

Oriental-inspired enameled mesh bag with silver-plated frame and twisted wire chain handle, marked Whiting and Davis.

Golden mesh and kid evening bag designed by Schiaparelli for Whiting and Davis, described as the "Evening bag of the moment in Paris." *Harper's Bazaar*, April, 1936.

The season's three smartest bags are after

Schiaparelli

by WHITING & DAVIS

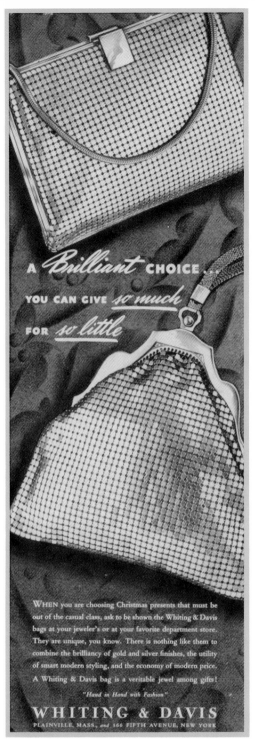

Ad for Whiting and Davis bags featured in *Harper's Bazaar*, December, 1939.

Large aluminum beadlite enamel mesh handbag with zippered closure, navy blue grosgrain lining, inside pocket with label that reads: "Alumesh Bags, Whiting and Davis Company."

White enameled mesh bag tipped in gold, made by Whiting and Davis. *Harper's Bazaar*, April, 1936.

Beadlite enamel (with a raised center resembling a bead) was also common in this decade. A two-toned "tile mesh bag", advertised in 1936, was made in the underarm style with a zippered closure and a lining of silk. The large beadlite mesh was enameled white and the raised bead section was tipped in gold.

Occasionally, enameled mesh bags of this vintage were made of aluminum. Because they were light weight, they sometimes assumed large dimensions. The labels found inside bags of this type read "Alumesh by Whiting and Davis."

During World War II, where the manufacture of mesh handbags was halted by war restrictions of certain metals, Whiting and Davis continued with items supporting the war effort. When normal production resumed, bright goldtone and silvertone armor mesh bags were made in abundance and they are extremely common today.

See additional advertisements for mesh bags on pages 174 to 177.

Black enameled Beadlite mesh hand-bag with Bakelite frame and handle, marked Whiting and Davis.

Aluminum beadlite mesh clutch bag with key chain attached to zipper pull, unmarked; goldtone beadlite mesh clutch with zippered closure, marked Whiting and Davis.

Envelope style clutch bag, belt, ear-rings and lipvues made of flat armor mesh by Whiting and Davis.

Three off-white beadlite enamel mesh bags by Whiting and Davis.

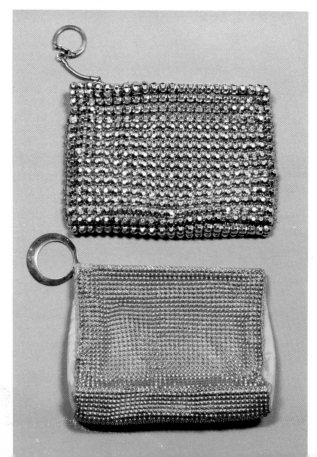

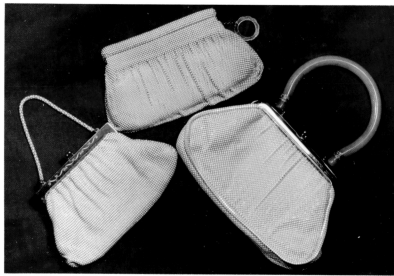

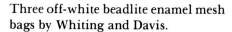

Silver-colored armor mesh handbag with jeweled frame, marked Whiting and Davis.

Whiting and Davis gold-colored armor mesh with gatetop frame and original presentation box.

Two gold-colored armor mesh bags with openwork frames, marked Whiting and Davis.

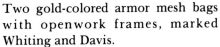

Small goldtone mesh bag with mesh strap handle and matching goldtone mesh collar made by Whiting and Davis.

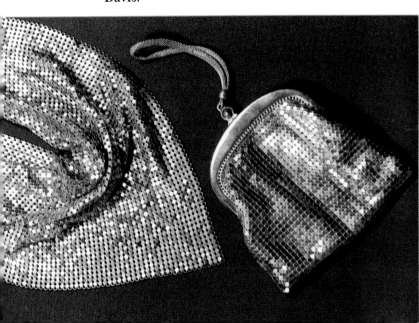

Sequin and lace evening bag with metal frame and chain handle.

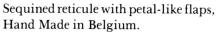

Sequined reticule with petal-like flaps, Hand Made in Belgium.

Black sequined bag attached to gold-tone gatetop frame. The inside label reads: "Hand Sewn Products, S. B. & Co."

Sequined pouch attached to goldtone gatetop expansion frame.

Chapter VI:

❧ Handbags of the 1930s

Many designers and manufacturers in the 1930s broadened their techniques in conjunction with the new materials that were being used in handbag manufacture. Tradition lent itself to innovation and a tremendous variety of handbags were put on the market. The Depression of the 1930s had an influence on the materials used in manufacture. American ingenuity began to surface as the country experienced economic instability. Luckily for Americans, however, this ingenuity would become extremely necessary in the next decade when war would force America to ''be on its own'' as far as fashion was concerned.

The average consumer of the thirties could not afford a handbag made of sterling silver much less of solid gold. Animal and reptile skins were still employed but many imitations were manufactured and sold through mail order catalogs and novelty stores at much lower prices. Plastics were abundant and sold at fractions of the cost of higher quality bags. Specific designers also leaned towards new dimensions in style as well as new materials used for their construction. For example, sling-like bags were designed by Paquin while satchels were designed by Suvianne. Marjorie Dunton created round and flat discus-type bags with chain handles while flat-bottomed bags were made by Aristocrat. Bags designed by Lewis displayed Monocraft metal monograms while Graceline Watch Bags, made of a new material called 'Celanese crepe Amcella', became the background for guaranteed time pieces mounted on the front of the handbag. Snakeskin bags tailored by Antoine were extremely fashionable while De Ravenel designed bags made of French antelope and an old favorite, Morocco leather.

Blue velvet pouch-type evening bag with snap closure and blue glass ring designed for hand carrying. The inside of the bag is lined with a lighter shade of blue satin, contains a shirred pocket fitted with small mirror.

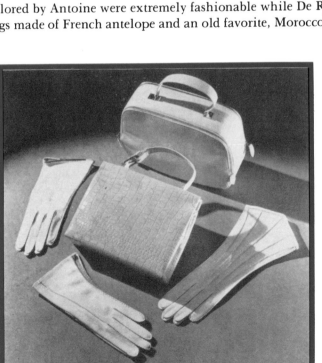

Aristocrat's alligator calf bag; Koret's lizard calf bag, *Harper's Bazaar*, circa 1937.

McCall's, April, 1932.

Imported handbags advertised for sale from Strawbridge and Clothier, December 1, 1930.

Summer handbags advertised in June, 1930.

Right UP TO THE SECOND

"Graceline" Watch Bags are designed for this mad gad-about world . . . where every second lost to fun is an eternity gone forever!

GRACELINE fashions these chic bags of lovely Celanese* Crepe Amcella, a perfect fabric complement to your spring ensembles. The colors and lines are as "right" as the trim-looking guaranteed time-piece with its new small face and unbreakable crystal. (*Reg. U. S. Pat. Off.)

You will like, too, the new "Kover-Zip" concealed automatic closing on certain models. "Graceline" Watch Bags are available in Navy, Beige, Grey, Black and Brown. Choice of styles at **$3**

Graceline

Graceline Watch Bags, circa 1936.

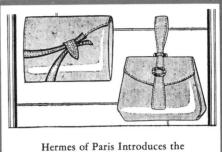

Hermes of Paris Introduces the

Natural Pigskin Handbag

*and Wanamaker's presents
exact copies at*

$7.50   **$10**

Hermes, saddler to Europe's nobility for nearly a hundred years, launches this smart fashion of the natural pigskin handbag for summer. Our copies are made of the finest imported natural pig . . . endless for wear, and easily cleaned. Soft as fabric bags, with their glove-snap clasps . . . rich linings of crimson, reseda green or black moire silk. Three back-strap envelopes at $7.50 . . . two underarms and a wrist-handle bag at $10.

Pigskin handbags by Hermes of Paris advertised in 1930.

Blue beaded bag adorned with working Swiss-made watch by Princess. The inside of the bag is lined in satin and stamped, "Hand Made in Belgium Exclusively for Sak's Fifth Avenue."

Chintz Sport Ensemble, circa 1930.

White grain calf bag designed by Schiaparelli advertised in *Harper's Bazaar*, April, 1936.

BAGS: 5. Shaped like an old-fashioned portmanteau—this black suède bag of Schiaparelli's, with a shiny plastic frame 6. Schiaparelli pulls off the suitcase trick again, in a bag of stiff red box-calf with a massive braided handle 7. Schiaparelli's pink kid evening bag, embossed with white flowers, shaped faintly like your grandmother's reticule 8. More of Schiaparelli's witticisms—this blue kid bag like an inverted stratosphere balloon. Enamel link handle 9. And this black box-calf bag with scooped-out sides 10. Suviane's pale blue velvet evening bag, suitcase-shaped and studded sparsely with brilliants, opens from either side

Schiaparelli and Suvianne handbags advertised in *Vogue*, July, 1937.

Envelope purse kit featured in *Needlecraft Magazine*, August, 1930.

Transfer designs for Italian quilted bags, McCall's Pattern Book, circa 1931.

Elsa Schiaparelli made a name for herself in this decade, not only with her fabulous fashions, but with her spectacular jewelry, her fun fragrances and her outlandish accessories. Her handbags were designed with a whimsical flair in addition to being clever and useful. She designed "old-fashioned portmanteau bags" made of suede and plastic as well as handbags that played music or lit up when opened. In 1937, Schiaparelli created a "shocking pink" kid leather evening bag which was enriched with embossed white flowers and advertised as a bag "shaped faintly like your grandmother's reticule." During this decade, a Victorian revival was evidenced in the manufacture of jewelry and clothing and because of this, many accessories, including purses and handbags were very reminiscent of nineteenth century reticules. Schiaparelli also designed a bag made of blue kid leather shaped like an inverted stratosphere balloon with an enamel link chain handle. She is also credited with renewing popularity in suede accessories in the 1930s. By designing a little suede cap, the craze for suede accessories caught on in Paris, New York and Hollywood. Designers used genuine dyed suede in bright colors or "ice cream pastels" such as lipstick red, raspberry, kelly green, summer blue, lemon, royal blue and aqua. Purses, hats, gloves and shoes were fashionable and sold at exclusive boutiques and fine department stores with extravagant price tags to match. The Handicraft Leather Company of Salem, Massachusetts sold mail-order kits called Kut-Ups which could be used to create your own suede accessories at home for fractions of the cost of the store bought items. One entire suede skin could be purchased for $2.00 in any of the above colors.

The French Bootery Company located in Chicago became noted for their lizard and suede combination handbags as well as their two-toned dyed

Bienen-Davis handbags advertised in *Harper's Bazaar*, April, 1936.

KORET INTRODUCES *"Carrot"* THE NEW COLOR FOR SPRING....

"CARROT" colors the season's smartest bags.... and changes the complexion of the whole spring style picture! It's another fashion first from Koret, who introduced the high style clay color two years ago. It's almost as important a new note as the clever styling of these handsome Handbag Originals!

SPRING SUIT SCOOP WITH THE NEW "CARROT" ACCESSORIES, FROM BONWIT TELLER.

THE MARK OF *a* KORET *Original*

snakeskin bags with matching shoes. Lujean of New York City manufactured straw handbags which were cheerfully decorated with clusters of fruit and vegetables, an extremely popular motif of the decade found on handbags and other accessories as well.

Bags made by Bienen-Davis, Incorporated of New York were high quality handbags that were very much in vogue in the mid-to-late thirties. Fine tailored examples were made of suede and calfskin with a superior quality and workmanship. All Bienen-Davis handbags were stamped with a little **b-d** monogram on the interior lining of the bag. These bags were sold at fine department stores.

Also on the list of popular handbags were those made by Koret. Calfskin bags were designed for day wear while quilted gold kid leather bags were fashioned for evening wear. In 1934, Koret introduced clay-colored handbags and in 1936, their Spring collection consisted of carrot-colored handbags. In 1939, they advertised their *Capriccio Espangnol* handbags. This particular line was made of lace accompanied by a matching lace fan. They were styled in the typical Spanish tradition inspired by the *Ballet Russe*.

Fashion publications throughout the decade were full of advertisements for handbags and accessories. Handbags were advertised as "chic and elegant" and different designer and manufacturer techniques accommodated this claim. Shirring and puckering were employed on cloth bags and soft pliable leather such as antelope. Pleating, piping, stitching and smocking were also common enrichments found on cloth and leather purses. Occasionally the same enrichments found on a particular dress, suit or coat were added to a matching handbag making a coordinating ensemble. This coordinating of accessories became the rage of the 1930s.

Envelope-style "pochettes" which were very modish in the teens and twenties continued to be fashionable throughout the entire decade. They were constantly referred to as back strap pouches, envelope style bags or underarm pouches and they were made of cloth, leather, leatherette or dyed suede. Beads, sequins and embroidery were common garnitures found on evening bags. Tailored envelope bags made of linen in subdued pastels were quite modish at this time in addition to smaller "pochettes" garnished with bugle beads and imitation pearls; the latter was offered in different styles and even different bead qualities. Shoulder bags became fashionable again as well as traditional top-handled purses. Bags made of felt were also in style.

Gold kid evening bag, shirred at jeweled frame, lined with satin, marked Harry Rosenfeld Original."

Zippered *pochette* made of black suede with dog motif made of white fur, goldtone metal ring used for carrying.

Opposite page:
Bags by Koret advertised in *Harper's Bazaar*, April, 1936.

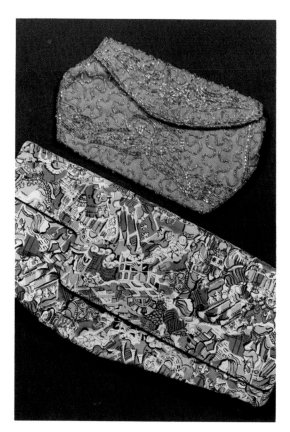

Salmon-colored gauze envelope style pouch decorated with clear beads (round and bugle), organdy lined, marked "Made in Belgium by hand, Walborg." Colorful abstract underarm bag, satin lined with one inside pocket.

Swagger handle bag and matching hat, circa 1930.

Talon Hookless Fasteners advertised in *The Ladies' Home Journal* June, 1933.

The "Swagger Handle" pouch bag was another predominant style of the 1930s. This type of handbag was frequently made of calfskin with a zippered closure called a "Talon Hookless Fastener." A loop handle, usually large enough to fit over the wrist, was attached to the zipper pull which enabled the woman to conveniently carry the purse. What made the Talon fastener catch on so quickly at this time was the fact that the handbags and purses no longer needed to be framed. The zipper now lent itself to flexibility of the purse and designers were able to be extremely creative in their designs. There was a tremendous amount of variety at this time due to these factors. Security was yet another factor stressed by the Talon Company. The zippered fastener was somewhat of a guarantee against loss of articles kept within the purse. Women did not have to worry about their purses opening up and articles falling out.

When handbags were framed, however, other materials besides metal were used. Prystal (clear plastic) frames, were used quite frequently during the 1930s in addition to more expensive frames made of clear crystal. Plastic frames were also made to look like amber, ivory, tortoiseshell and mother of pearl. The plastic could also be molded to resemble hand carved work which was usually done on ivory. Metal frames displayed decorative techniques such as enameling, embossing and engraving. Electroplating added elegant touches to inexpensive base metals and studding with rhinestones also added class to a relatively inexpensive evening bag.

Patent leather was in vogue at that time and was made available in various colors such as navy blue, green, red, black and white. Frameless pouches with Talon fasteners were made of patent leather in addition to traditional top-handled handbags. Imitation patent leather was also offered and the price was exceptionally modest.

Purple grosgrain bag attached to Prystal frame.

Black grosgrain pouch-type bag with Prystal cathedral dome-style frame and black ribbon handle.

Harper's Bazaar April, 1936.

three loves .. an exclusive new Paris-designed bag of soft crush cape encircled with three gold wedding bands. In 17 different colors including white. **$10.**

425 FIFTH AVENUE · NEW YORK

No. 7592-18, Envelope Pouch of pochette calf, black, brown, or blue, $7.50.

No. 1046-13, side handle Envelope, shrunken calf, black or brown, $10.

Rolf's La Garde handbags advertised in 1936.

Medieval-style hand-stitched bag by Jodelle, *Harper's Bazaar* April, 1936.

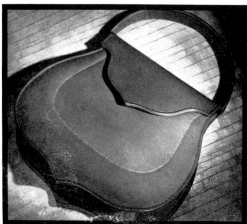

In 1936, Rolf's of New York City advertised their original "La Garde" handbags which were hand-crafted in top grain leather and equipped with Talon hookless fasteners and expanding gusseted pockets. Made in the envelope style, top handle or swagger pouch variety, they were priced from $5.00 and up and sold at the better stores. Rolf's was a division of Amity Leather Products of West Bend, Wisconsin which was responsible for making key cases, billfolds and cigarette cases crafted in fine leather.

In the same year, medieval styled pouch-type bags were designed by Jodelle. The navy blue calf was hand-stitched to resemble "the ones they wore with doublet and hose-and so often carried poison in—in the stirring times of Henri III and the Medicis."

Bags designed by Miss Penn were quite unique in 1936 and advertised as patented novelty handbags. They were designed with a "hideaway cigarette compartment" which created quite a novelty at that time. In 1937, fitted handbags (designed to hold cosmetic cases) were styled by Elizabeth Arden and Helena Rubinstein.

Evening bags were still popularly fashioned in metal mesh by Whiting and Davis and Mandalian in addition to gold chain mail bags designed by Volokhoff. Other fancy bags designed specifically for evening wear were made of sumptuous Persian brocade, crocheted gold metallic thread, black suede or velvet enriched with rhinestones, marcasites or iridescent crystals. Needlepoint, petit point, beaded or tambour embroidered bags were still imported from Austria, France, Belgium and Czechoslovakia and highly fashionable.

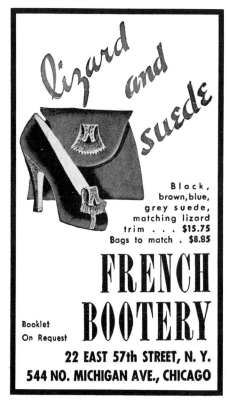
Harper's Bazaar, November, 1937.

Harper's Bazaar August, 1936.

Black velvet evening bag enriched with a single row of square-cut rhinestones mounted in gilded lift lock. The inside of the bag is lined with off-white satin, fitted with mirror, comb and attached coin purse.

Hand braided leather bags sold through the Sears catalogue in 1937.

In 1939, advertisements for coordinating shoes and handbags made of 'Largarto' were prominent in leading fashion magazines. Largarto, which was referred to as a small reptile with skin that resembled ''priceless mosaics in miniature'' were crafted by Andrew Geller of New York.

The list of prominent designers and popular manufacturers during this innovative decade could go on and on. Mail order companies such as Sears, Roebuck and Company and Montgomery Ward also offered a very large selection of purses and handbags at much lower prices. For example, black, brown, green or wine-colored suede handbags with prystal handles and trims sold for $2.98 from Montgomery Ward in 1937. Hand braided bags of genuine leather were also fashionable and they too were constructed with the popular zippered fastener, a rayon lining and two inside compartments fitted with a mirror. Wards sold this variety for ninety-eight cents. Durable steerhide bags, either hand-tooled or embossed, were still quite modish and they were designed in the top handle and back strap variety retailing for $2.98 and up.

Sears, Roebuck and Company offered a large selection of unusual as well as traditional favorites at very affordable prices. All-white ''Rodalac'' composition handbags, which were ivory-like, resembling celluloid, were available in many styles and qualities ranging in price from ninety-four cents to $1.98 each. Sears also sold ''pearlite'' handbags made of a soft leather-like material displaying a satiny luster of pearls. Available in a choice of colors to include white, pink, light blue, maize and lilac, these bags retailed for $1.79 in 1937. Another celluloid composition offered by Sears was a material called ''crystaloid.'' This composition was used for making very inexpensive handbags which sold for as low as thirty-nine cents each.

Wooden beaded bag colored in Mexican stripes with celluloid frame and link chain handle.

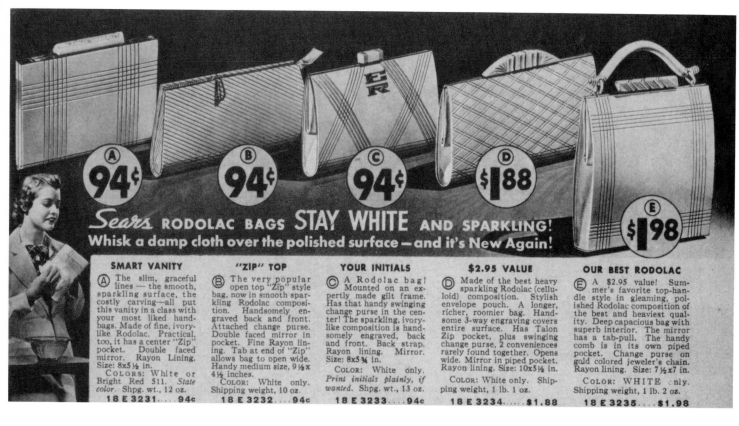

SMART VANITY

(A) The slim, graceful lines — the smooth, sparkling surface, the costly carving—all put this vanity in a class with your most liked handbags. Made of fine, ivory-like Rodolac. Practical, too, it has a center "Zip" pocket. Double faced mirror. Rayon Lining. Size: 8x5½ in.

COLORS: White or Bright Red 511. *State color.* Shpg. wt., 12 oz.

18 E 3231 ... 94c

"ZIP" TOP

(B) The very popular open top "Zip" style bag, now in smooth sparkling Rodolac composition. Handsomely engraved back and front. Attached change purse. Double faced mirror in pocket. Fine Rayon lining. Tab at end of "Zip" allows bag to open wide. Handy medium size, 9½x 4½ inches.

COLOR: White only. Shipping weight, 10 oz.

18 E 3232 ... 94c

YOUR INITIALS

(C) A Rodolac bag! Mounted on an expertly made gilt frame. Has that handy swinging change purse in the center! The sparkling, ivory-like composition is handsomely engraved, back and front. Back strap. Rayon lining. Mirror. Size: 8x5¾ in.

COLOR: White only. *Print initials plainly, if wanted.* Shpg. wt., 13 oz.

18 E 3233 ... 94c

$2.95 VALUE

(D) Made of the best heavy sparkling Rodolac (celluloid) composition. Stylish envelope pouch. A longer, richer, roomier bag. Handsome 3-way engraving covers entire surface. Has Talon Zip pocket, plus swinging change purse, 2 conveniences rarely found together. Opens wide. Mirror in piped pocket. Rayon lining. Size: 10x5½ in.

COLOR: White only. Shipping weight, 1 lb. 1 oz.

18 E 3234 ..... $1.88

OUR BEST RODOLAC

(E) A $2.95 value! Summer's favorite top-handle style in gleaming, polished Rodolac composition of the best and heaviest quality. Deep capacious bag with superb interior. The mirror has a tab-pull. The handy comb is in its own piped pocket. Change purse on gold colored jeweler's chain. Rayon lining. Size: 7½x7 in.

COLOR: WHITE only. Shipping weight, 1 lb. 2 oz.

18 E 3235 ... $1.98

Sears' Rodolac bags offered for sale in 1937.

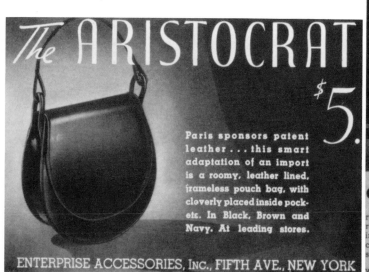

Vogue May, 1938.

Sears For Imported Wood Bead Bags!

THEY'RE SMART ... THEY'RE PRACTICAL ... THEY'RE EASILY CLEANED

94c Handmade of imported enameled wood beads that resist soiling. Zip top! Mirror. Rayon lining. Size: 7x4 in. COLORS: White or Multicolored Mexican peasant stripes. *State color.*
18 E 3240—Shipping weight, 7 ounces.

$1.88 Larger size! Zip top style! Handmade of imported enameled wood beads. Mirror in pocket. Rayon lining. Size: 9½x5 in. COLORS: White or Multicolored Mexican peasant stripes. *State color.*
18 E 3241—Shipping weight, 10 ounces.

$1.88 Fashionable top-handle style. Handmade of enameled wood beads. Talon top. Mirror in pocket. Rayon lining. Size: 9½x5½ in. COLORS: White or gay Multi-colored Mexican peasant stripes. *State color.*
18 E 3242—Shipping weight, 12 ounces.

Sears wooden beaded bags offered for sale in 1937.

Imported enameled wooden beaded bags with rayon linings were also quite a novelty at this time. In 1937, this type of bag sold for ninety-four cents to $1.88 depending on its size. They were available in white or multi-colored Mexican peasant stripes.

For $1.00 each, one could purchase a Sears famous "Vachelle" handbag which was advertised as the "developed, cleanable handbag material." Obviously their best quality imitation leather, this new material was used for designing envelope style, swagger style and top-handled bags with zippered closures and visible embossed designs creating many desirable effects. The purses came equipped with inside coin purses and mirrors. Sears stated that these bags were copies of better bags sold at fine department stores.

Hand crocheted rayon handbags with matching belts and gloves were also popular and reasonably priced. Sears offered these coordinating sets in white, navy blue or maize for $1.53. Bags called "Doeskin", made of lamb suede, were also stylish and priced at $1.49 each.

In 1938, Sears sold triangular, rectangular, fan or crescent-shaped handbags made of seal, calf and morocco-grained Vachelle. Zippered closures, ring closures and knob clasps were used. These inexpensive copies of more costly bags sold for eighty-nine cents each. They also sold bags made of genuine calf leather, seal leather, crushed goat-hide and buffalo leather in black, India brown and navy blue for $2.95 and $4.95 each. Available with rough or fine-grained textures and leather linings, they were called "Treasure-Craft Bags."

Hand crocheted rayon frill ensemble offered from Sears in 1937.

| Two Crown "Zips" at top make 2 separate roomy sections. In Morocco grained Vachelle, the developed handbag material. Coin purse, mirror. Initials included. Size, 9¾ x 7½ in. **Colors:** Black, Navy Blue or Brown 909. **State color; print 2 initials.** 18 K 3450—Shipping weight, 15 ounces. 89¢ | Crown "Zip" closing in this handsome bag of calf-grained Vachelle, the smart handbag material. Costly-looking stitched effect at front. Coin purse, mirror. Size, 10¼ x 9 in. **Colors:** Black, Navy Blue or Brown Copper 913. **State color.** 18 K 3451—Shipping weight, 1 lb. 1 oz. 89¢ | Crown "Zip" top in this beautifully designed bag. Graceful pleats at front. Made of handsome Morocco grained Vachelle. Mirror and coin purse. Roomy interior. Size, 10 x 7 in. **Colors:** Black, Navy Blue or India Brown 909. **State color.** 18 K 3452—Shipping weight, 15 ounces. 89¢ | Dainty and dressy bag with fan like pleats front and back. The deep frame opens wide. In calf-grained Vachelle handbag material. Coin purse, mirror. Size, 11½ x 7½ in. **Colors:** Black, India Brown 909, Purple Plum 912. **State color.** 18 K 3453—Shipping weight, 1 lb. 1 oz. 89¢ | Smart, square bag of Seal grained Vachelle, the developed handbag material. Neatly pleated front. Rayon lining coin purse, mirror. Size, 9¾ x 8¾ in. **Colors:** Black, Navy Blue or India Brown 909. **State color.** 18 K 3454—Shipping weight, 1 lb. 4 oz. 89¢ |

Handbags featured in the 1938/1939 Fall and Winter Sears catalogue.

Black grosgrain box bag enriched with engraved goldtone frame.

Butler Brothers, a wholesale company, displayed a wide variety of handbags and purses for women and children in 1937. Most of these bags were made from a material called "Keratol." Keratol was a coated waterproof material similar to vinyl which was grained to look like genuine leather. The envelope style, underarm style and popular vanity style bags were offered. An 8½" by 5½" underarm style bag designed with a back strap and inside mirror wholesaled for $2.10 per dozen with a single retail price of twenty-five cents. The Keratol bags were available in different grained effects and the catalog stated that "calf, alligator and beaver grain are the important handbag fabrics for street and daytime wear." Silk and velvet bags were the appropriate choices for evening wear. Bags were designed with pleated fronts, novelty clasps, unusual handles, metal frames and zippered frameless pouches. Children's purses were similarly styled with added novelty trims suited for the young person. A 2½" by 2¼" Keratol bag made with a metal frame and chain handle, decorated with a watch ornament, sold for ten cents. Other novel decorations included bears, dogs, birds, boats and bows.

Innovation and ingenuity throughout this decade was evidenced by the tremendous amounts of synthetic plastics and imitation leathers that were creatively employed in handbag manufacture. With an unstable economy throughout most of this decade, manufacturers were still able to cater to the whims of women from all walks of life.

See additional advertisements for handbags of the nineteen thirties on pages 178 to 180.

Grey broadcloth bag with knob clasp.

Two crocheted gimp bags attached to plastic frames.

William Wilder purses advertised in 1937.

Brown broadcloth bag with clear plastic lift lock.

McCall's, February, 1938.

Handwoven leather back strap pouch with loop and button fastener, silk lining, marked "Hand Woven Leather Bags, Aug. 16, 1932." Black handwoven suede top-handled bag with zippered closure and imitation leather lining.

Brown suede handbag with gold-plated clasp, satin lined, marked "Koret, Koretolope Made of Non-Crockable Kid Suede."

Large underarm bag made of multi-colored rows of braided gimp fashioned in Mexican Peasant stripes attached to carved wooden frame.

Black broadcloth handbag with molded plastic frontpiece, set with colored glass stones, satin lined, stamped "Guild Creations."

Chocolate brown woolen broadcloth bag accented with beadwork, panier handle, lined in dark brown grosgrain cloth, marked "K & G, Charlet Bag, Paris, New York."

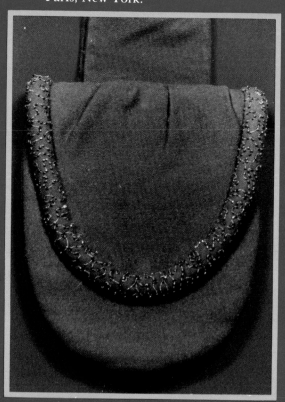

Chapter VII:

❧ Handbags of the 1940s

Emerging from the Great Depression and thrusting directly into a second world war, manufacturing during the early forties was very unstable. Consequently, war restrictions on certain metals swayed designers and manufacturers to utilize other materials. Zippers and metal purse frames were extremely scarce and were often replaced by wood which was used for framing large envelope-style underarm bags. The wood was offered as either smooth or "richly carved." Lift lock closures, made of early plastics, and loop and button fasteners were used to a large degree at this time. Drawstring reticules were again an integral part of the fashion scene. Prices for specific designer handbags rose dramatically, especially those made of genuine leather and taxes were imposed on costume jewelry and accessories.

In 1940, Schiaparelli was still designing unusual handbags made of box calf and antelope leather in addition to a revolutionary material known as "rhodophane" which was transparent like glass.

Lucien Lelong created unusual box calf handbags stitched in white with a circle of clear cellophane attached to the outside of the bag. This clear pocket could be used for a variety of purposes like holding a pretty pair of gloves or a fancy handkerchief and it added a decorative touch.

Cristobal Balenciaga designed quilted, black antelope money bags to swing from the wrist (panier handle) in addition to black taffeta and ribbon drawstring evening bags.

Molyneux created a bag in the shape of a half moon made of "brown silk surah with yellow polka dots." These choice designer bags were rather costly at the time and only available in fine department stores. Similar versions, however, were copied and produced in imitation leathers and lower quality fabrics with equally low price tags.

Contour bags were designed by Josef made of "suedera" which was a Forstmann's broadcloth composed of 40% cashmere and 60% virgin wool. This combination created a luxurious fabric which was then dyed in many different colors to continue the trend of coordinating outfits. Suedera bags by Josef were decorated with 24K gold-plated trims and retailed for $18.50 to $35.00 and up in the mid-to-late forties.

S.Steinman originals were elegant designer handbags also made in Forstmann's broadcloth or dyed calfskin. Sold in fine department stores, these bags retailed for about $40. Less expensive copies made of Botany brand broadcloth or faille could be purchased for about $10. Jenny bags were designed as over-the-arm contoured pouches. They were made of an inexpensive broadcloth retailing for about $12.50.

Antelope vanity box-bag with goldtone metal frame. The inside is equipped with large mirror, comb and shirred pocket to hold cosmetics.

Black cashmere broadcloth bag with goldtone frame, satin lining, marked "Fabrigue Made In USA."

S.Steinman Original, circa 1947.

Black virgin wool bag with double handles and plastic frame decorated with crest design. The inside of the bag is lined in silk with three pockets fitted with mirror, comb and coin purse, marked "Lewis 100% Virgin Wool."

Jenny Bags, *Vogue* September, 1947.

CONTAINERS for eggs, cheese, wine and fish are the humble objects from which smart handbags are made.

Life March 29, 1948.

American ingenuity continued to flourish and in the second half of this particular decade, unusual basket and wooden box bags became the newest fad. Cheese, wine, fish and egg containers were cleverly decorated with colored canvas, leather, corduroy and metal trim. These bags seemed to be the rage in 1948 when they were sold on Fifth Avenue in New York City. Prices ranged from $10.00 to $20.00 each. The vogue for this type of bag was short-lived since the novelty wore off in a few years.

A fad which was not so ephemeral was a handmade bag crocheted with gimp or corde'. Although bags of this type were beginning to surface in the late thirties, they did not reach their peak until the early forties. Pattern books were plentiful with dozens of styles to choose from. Women, once again, resorted to their handwork skills. Step by step instructions were given in order to crochet handbags and matching hats using either gimp or corde'. Each bag was given a different name such as the "Hollywood Bag", the "Crest Bag", the "Monogram Bag" and the "Crossways Bag." The bags were almost always framed in plastic or unframed with zipper closures and plastic zipper pulls. Occasionally, this type of bag had a metal frame attached but this was probably the result of an older frame being put to use on a modern bag. Drawstring reticule style bags were also constructed of crocheted gimp or corde' and sometimes further embellished with beadwork.

Two crocheted gimp bags fashioned in shell stitch. The bag on the top is attached to carved ivory frame.

Unfinished crocheted bag fashioned in popular shell stitch.

"Venetian Bag" crocheted with gimp using single crochet and cable stitch, circa 1940.

"Crossways Bag" crocheted with gimp using single, double and treble crochet, circa 1940.

Crocheted gimp bag attached to metal frame.

"Frame Shell Bag" and "Moonbeam Bag" crocheted with gimp, circa 1940.

The large fan-shaped gimp and corde' handbags were designed to employ clear plastic bracelet handles, sometimes spiraled, in addition to clear plastic ornaments attached to the end of the zipper pull. Different crochet stitches were used to create different patterns making each bag unique. The shell stitch was extremely common on small handbags that were attached to lightweight plastic frames. The frames were sometimes molded with bird designs, flowers and leaves. Single, double and treble crochet stitches were also used. These bags were extremely durable and when found in today's market, the majority are still in excellent condition.

Commercially-made corde' handbags consisted of rows of gimp stitched to a fabric background creating extremely unique patterns. In the early forties, Sears offered their "original rayon corde' fabric intricately stitched row on row" creating wonderful handbags which retailed for $7.50 each. They were designed in the underarm pouch and wrist styles with prystal (clear plastic) pulls and lift locks. Advertised as the "dressiest, handsomest and longest-wearing of all handbag fabrics", this promise really held true. Corde' bags were designed for winter wear. In 1949, Sears offered corde' bags that were further accented with flower quilting. These bags sold for $8.98.

Black corde' bag with Talon fastener, Prystal zipper pull and spiraled Prystal handles.

Large brown corde' bag with two spiraled Prystal handles.

Collection of five miniature purses all designed to be worn as necklaces. *Amber Lee Ettinger.*

Corde' bag with Prystal handles, circa 1946.

Corde' hat and bag, circa 1940.

Commercially-made black corde' envelope style bag and swagger handle bag marked Genuine Corde'.

Commercially-made brown corde' panier handle bag with imitation tortoiseshell frame.

Genuine corde' bags sold through the Sears catalogue in 1943.

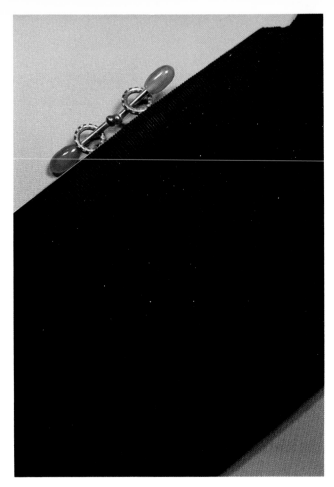

Large black corded fabric underarm
bag accented with Bakelite.

Commercially-made black corde' bag
with Prystal handles and zipper pull.
The inside of the bag had a cloth label
that reads: "Genuine Corde'."

Imitation corde' bags also became a large part of the Sears inventory.
"Corded" fabrics of durable cotton and rayon were made into handbags with
zippered closures. Large and small underarm pouches and top-handled bags
were designed in corded fabric, either solid black, brown or a "brilliant
blended multi-color." Corduroy shoulder bags were also sold through Sears
and they retailed for less than $2.00 each. In 1942, richly textured cloth bags,
either embroidered or beaded were styled with carved wooden frames and
handles. Purses made of removable linen slip covers were quite fashionable
and advertised as easy to keep clean.

Imitation leather handbags were also sold through the Sears catalog in
varying qualities. For example, a simulated leather bag with a snap closure
sold for sixty-nine cents in 1942. A little better quality imitation with a
zippered closure sold for $1.00 while the best quality imitation leather with a
combination of a zipper and a snap closure sold for $1.59. The same held true
for patent leather. A good bag of simulated patent leather with a knob clasp
made in the underarm pouch style sold for $1.00; the better model containing
an amber-like clasp sold for $1.59; while the largest and best quality of all sold
for $1.95.

Handbags made with square tiles of lightweight plastic linked with plain
or multi-colored lacing were referred to as "plastiflex" bags in 1942. These
bags were designed in the large underarm pouch style with navy blue linings
and zippered closures. They retailed for $2.95 and were designed for summer
wear. By 1948, Spiegel offered the same type of bag for $2.38. Lightweight
plaques of natural wood were styled in the same fashion and offered in 1944
for $4.95.

Spring and Summer bags featured in
the 1942 Sears catalogue.

Guaranteed cleanable **$2.95** Each

Genuine Plasticflex
Flexible; gleams like new with each cleansing. Zip top. Navy Rayon lining. Mirror; change purse. White with White or Multi-color lacing. State choice. Shipping weight, 1 pound 2 ounces.

Our Finest Supple Leather
Cleans quickly with a damp cloth . . . processed to wear better. Full length zip opens wide. Change purse, mirror. Navy rayon lining. Colors: White or Navy. State color. Shipping weight, 1 pound 5 ounces.

Cool, snow-white square "tiles" of light-weight plastic . . . linked with white or multi-color patent-like lacing.

Sears, Roebuck and Company, circa 1942.

McCall's March, 1943.

Envelope bag and matching beret made of wool and cotton felt, circa 1943.

Alligator-grained calf bags retailing for $4.88 each in the 1943 Sears catalogue.

In 1943, Sears sold fine leather handbags which were styled by leading American designers. Extremely long underarm bags were styled by *Mam'sellee* made of goat leather and lined with rayon. They possessed a "tailored look that's classic for suits..." These designer bags retailed for $7.50. Another line of Sears handbags was trademarked "Charmode" bags. Made of top grain saddle cowhide and small grained lambskin, they were designed in the underarm envelope style and the over-the-shoulder bag. They were also lined with rayon and sold for $4.88 each.

In the 1943-1944 Sears catalog, small footnotes appeared at the bottom of select pages informing the consumer that "zippers and closures in handbags were made before government restrictions on the use of metals. Construction may change slightly when present stocks are exhausted." Styles of handbags changed very little in subsequent catalogs with the exception of a growing trend towards the drawstring reticule, and a tremendous use of fabric, wood and plastic.

In 1946, "Kerrybrooke" leather bags (another Sears trademark) were higher quality leather bags than those offered in the past. These bags were designed in the swagger style, the twin top handle, twin zip underarm and the fitted envelope style. They were made of carefully selected, unscarred goatskin leather. The best quality of rayon was used for the lining and jam-proof zippers, knob clasps and snaps were used for closures.

Bags made of rayon faille were extremely popular in this decade in addition to those made of colored felt. Curled rayon pile was particularly fashionable at that time because this man-made fabric resembled Persian lamb. Handbags, muffs and hats were fashioned from this expensive-looking fabric. Shirring

Sears, circa 1943.   Sears, circa 1946.

Curled rayon pile hat and muff bag, Sears, 1946.

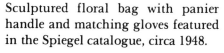

Boxy handbags featured in the Spiegel catalogue in 1948.

Sculptured floral bag with panier handle and matching gloves featured in the Spiegel catalogue, circa 1948.

Cotton eyelet drawstring pouch and matching gloves, Spiegel, 1948.

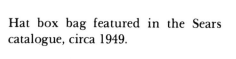

Hat box bag featured in the Sears catalogue, circa 1949.

Black silk hat box bag with goldtone monogram on top. The inside of the bag is lined with silk, fitted with a large mirror, marked "Bonwit Teller, Fifth Avenue, New York."

Vinylite handbag, circa 1947.

and puckering were still common on cloth and leather bags in addition to riveting metal ornaments and studding with imitation gemstones. Bracelet handle bags made with spiraled prystal were fashioned not only on corde' and gimp handbags, but on imitation corded fabric bags as well. New "boxy handbags" were beginning to surface which would set the pace for the next decade. Spiegel offered a few varieties in 1948. "The Hat Box Bag" was a new oval-shaped box-type bag made of plastic calf or rayon faille. It contained a round vanity mirror in the lid. "The Beau Bandbox" was an evening bag with a "flirty tied handle." It was large enough to hold a "full quota of date-time paraphernalia." Made of rayon faille and decorated with a "highly polished metal frame", it sold for $2.38.

When World War II came to an end, many technological advances began to occur especially in the production and perfection of modern plastics. A new flexible material called "koroseal" was made available by the B.F.Goodrich Company of Akron, Ohio. Koroseal was 100% waterproof, stain resistant and crack resistant. It did not peel and it was also guaranteed not to turn brittle, as was the fate of some of the earlier plastics. Handbags made in dozens of shapes, sizes and colors were offered and sold in better stores for $5.00 in the late forties. Handbags and other articles made of koroseal were advertised as "the smartest things in postwar styling..." Aprons, luggage, suspenders, belts, umbrellas, garment bags, shower curtains, draperies and marine upholstery were also made of this revolutionary material.

At the same time, the Bakelite Corporation, a subsidiary of Union Carbide and Carbon Corporation, marketed another new plastic with the tradename of "vinylite." This advanced material was also waterproof, mildew and weather resistant. It resisted scuffs, scratches and was extremely durable. All of these characteristics made this product a likely candidate for use in the manufacture of modern handbags.

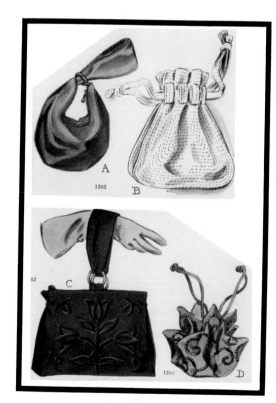

McCall's, circa 1949.

See additional advertisements for handbags of the nineteen forties on page 180.

Koroseal handbags advertised in *Life* on December 8, 1947.

Ivory-colored pearlized plastic bag with triangular shaped clasp, double handles, inside mirror, marked "Shell-Glow by Simplex."

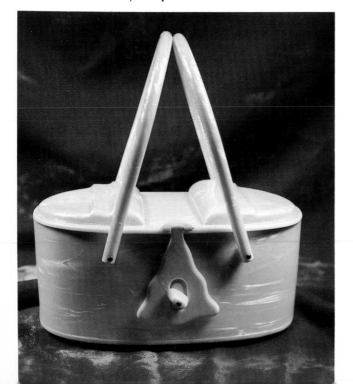

Pearlized plastic handbag with filigree flower ornament on lift lock, marked Wilardy.

Chapter VIII:

❧ Handbags of the 1950s

In the late forties, postwar technology was also responsible for perfecting a plastic called "lucite." This new material possessed an extremely modern appearance in comparison to the traditional materials used for previous handbag manufacture. Surpassing koroseal and vinylite, lucite was the perfect choice for making box-type handbags that were becoming extremely fashionable at this time. The lucite that was used for these boxy purses could be made transparent, translucent or opaque. The bags were decorated with gemstones, shells, confetti, glitter, flowers, lace and filigree ornamentation. Unusual shapes were common and this new type of handbag created a sensation, especially in big cities like Miami and New York City where most of the manufacture of these ultra modern handbags took place. These bags possessed an unusually modernistic quality that made them so unique and popular. They were fashionable for over ten years beginning in the late forties, yet practically disappeared by 1960. Lucite handbags came in all shapes, sizes, colors and textures and were worn by all ages from the sophisticated lady to the young teenie bopper.

Clear lucite clutch lined with white cloth.

Clear lucite handbag studded with rhinestones with attached hinged handle.

Octagonal-shaped speckled lucite handbag.

Amber-colored plastic handbag with lace-lined lid and stationary handle.

Pearlized plastic handbag enriched with pierced goldtone band.

Clear lucite bag marked Gilli Originals, New York.

Wilardy in New York seemed to manufacture the most exquisite and most expensive examples of lucite bags which were sold in fine department stores nationwide. Many other companies, however, manufactured cheaper versions which were sold in novelty stores at fractions of the cost of the sophisticated designer bags. Other top manufacturers were Rialto, Llewllyn, Gilli Originals, Patricia of Miami, Evans, Myles and Maxim. Almost all of the bags made by the top of the line manufacturers are marked on the inside of the bag; the mark can be found either stamped on the metal frame or accompanied by a transparent label. Unfortunately, many of these labels have fallen off through the years and identification becomes dubious. Most of the generic equivalents were never marked casting uncertainty about their origins. In any case, today these lucite bags have become extremely collectible and as a result, prices have sky-rocketed. Ironically, certain top of the line designer bags, back in the fifties, sold for over $50.00 each, an extravagant sum to pay for a plastic purse forty years ago. Lucite bags have a certain charm all of their own; typically a fifties style which has become a nineties collectible.

There were many other popular styles in the fifties besides lucite purses. For instance, bright colored leather and dyed suede handbags were very stylish, especially when accompanied by matching shoes, belts or hats. Gloves were also preferred at this time to complete the overall look and create an ensemble. Gloves in related pastel shades were appropriate. Llama calf was another modish leather as well as alligator and crocodile handbags particularly styled in the shoulder bags variety or the traditional top-handled bag. Also during this decade, a name change occurred and envelope style underarm bags were now called clutch bags.

Confetti-type lucite bag accented with rhinestones, marked Patricia of Miami.

Plastic clutch bag accented with black net and gold thread. The frame is covered in gold kid leather with molded plastic ornament across the front.

Heavy acetate handbag made to resemble tortoiseshell, marked Tyrolean, New York.

This wooden bag is further ornamented with a plastic top hand-painted with a Spanish theme. The wooden bottom is decorated with ribbon, braid and metallic thread in a woven design.

A clear lucite top and handle is attached to this unusual metallic red plastic bottom making a very unique bag.

Thin sheets of lightweight plastic decorated with rhinestones, imitation pearls and molded plastic flowers surround this basket-type bag with attached wooden handle. The bottom of the bag is covered in a brocaded fabric.

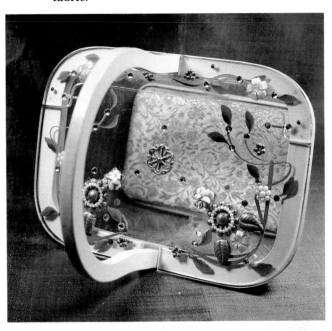

Hat and Bag ensembles, circa 1953.

Two lace clutch bags with zippered closures.

Two small evening bags made of satin, covered with net and studded with rhinestones. *Amber Lee Ettinger*.

Two envelope style clutch bags made of velvet, brocade and gold net, marked Majestic.

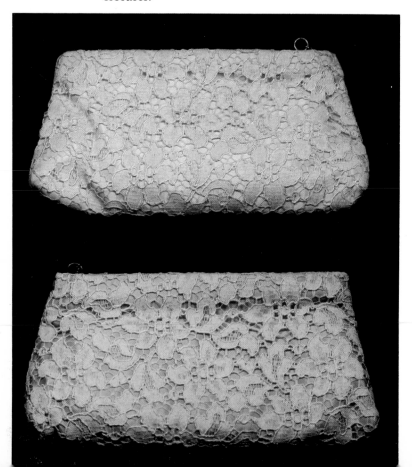

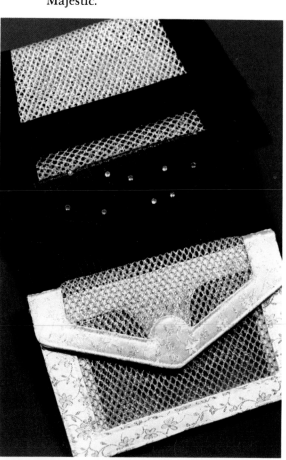

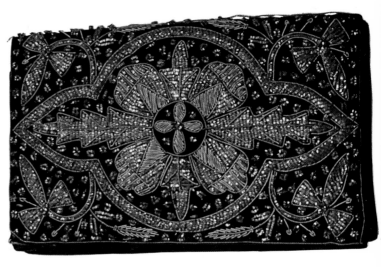

Bag and Glove Sets made of cotton eyelet, rayon faille and cotton pique, Spiegel, 1951.

Black silk clutch bag embellished with metallic embroidery, Made In India.

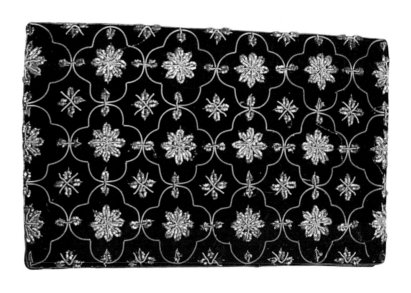

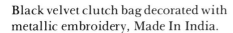

Black velvet clutch bag decorated with metallic embroidery, Made In India.

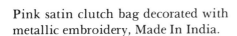

Pink satin clutch bag decorated with metallic embroidery, Made In India.

Drawstring bag, circa 1953.

In 1951, the Spiegel catalog offered more handbags made of plastic than that of any other material. Since corde' was still in vogue, plastic handbags, embossed to look like genuine corde', were manufactured and they retailed for $1.98 each. Plastic patent, plastic calf and crown jewel plastic were the most popular types offered in this catalog. Handbags in dozens of shapes and sizes were made from these plastic imitations. Drawstring pouches were again stylish and were available in matched sets with coordinating gloves. They were constructed of washable cotton eyelet, rayon faille and cotton pique, retailing for about $3.50 per set and popular for summer wear. "Bag and Glove Match Mates" were also sold through the Sears catalog made of rayon velvet studded with sequins or sueded rayon which was pleated and popular for winter wear.

In the same year, Sears offered what they called their "Curtain Rod Bag." By loosening the screws on the bag's plastic frame and removing the gold-colored metal rods, the rayon cover would slip from the frame and was ready for laundering. Beadette bags were also stylish in this period. They were made of sturdy pastel or deep-colored plastic beads, usually glued onto a gabardine twill. They were sometimes referred to as "caviar beaded bags" and were most often designed in the drawstring pouch style, the top-handled snap bag or the zippered fastener pouch or clutch type bags. Occasionally offered in the framed variety, some were reversible with different colored beading on both sides.

Handbags made of plastic coil were also in vogue in the fifties. These bags were available in solid white, black and white combination, or multi-colored and they retailed for less than $4.00. Clutch bags and shoulder bags were popular in this style.

Hat and matching bag, circa 1953.

Imitation corde' bag made of white plastic lined in blue faille.

Multi-colored Caviar beaded pouch with zippered closure.

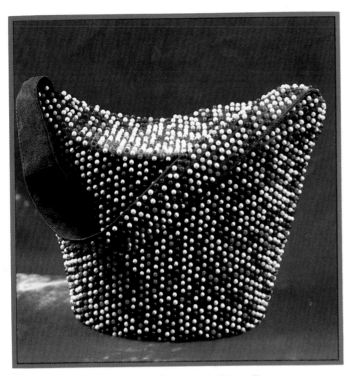

Multi-colored Caviar beaded handbag with flap closure.

Caviar beaded bag made in the drawstring style.

Plastic beads decorate these 1950s gatetop purses. *Amber Lee Ettinger.*

Black plastic coil handbag with zippered closure.

Black and white plastic coiled clutch
bag with enameled frame.

Plastic coil shoulder bag with zippered
closure and coil zipper pull.

Hand-tooled leather bag with
adjustable shoulder strap.

Hand-tooled black leather shoulder
bag.

Hand tooled leather bags were again seen in mail order catalogs in the early fifties. Montgomery Ward sold "Hand Made Guatemalan Imports" made of cowhide with a shoulder strap for $8.98 in 1953. Sears sold the same bag two years earlier for twenty cents less. By 1955, Sears referred to these same bags as "authentic ranch-styled" made of top grain cowhide by "Western Cowboy Craftsmen" and designed in the adjustable shoulder strap variety. This time they retailed for $15.98 each. They were all hand-laced and hand-tooled with floral patterns available in all saddle tan or two-toned (natural tan with dark brown).

The fifties became the decade for the rage in boxy-type handbags. As mentioned earlier, the lucite bags were very fashionable but extensive research through period catalogs displays very few of them. Instead, the catalogs presented boxy handbags made of velvet, rayon faille, plastic calf, plastic puffet, dacron, cubed plastic, polished calf, sueded rayon, corde', acetate faille, gold-colored metal filigree and many others. One exception was a molded plastic box bag made of clear, pearl-like or tortoise shell-like plastic which was advertised in the 1953 Spiegel catalog. It retailed for $2.38. The expensive designer lucite bags were obviously only sold in boutiques and fine department stores while the low end imitations were sold through wholesale catalogs or found in novelty stores.

The Oval Box in genuine snakeskin

$6.00 Tax included

Luxurious, exciting snakeskin, the fashion-right leather for spring, is ideal for this dramatic oval box. Gleaming gold-color metal frame opens wide. Sturdy rayon lining. Mirror. About 7x4 in. Shipping wt. 1 lb. 2 oz.
88 K 668E—Brown   88 K 669E—Red
88 K 670E—Green   Each.... $6.00

Oval box bag made of snakeskin, circa 1951.

Genuine alligator and top grain cowhide bags featured in the 1955 Sears catalogue.

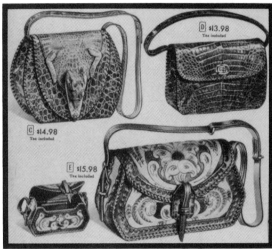

Multi-colored beaded bag accented with goldtone trim, beaded handles, faille lining and large inside mirror.

Alligator handbags continued to be popular, especially in the adjustable shoulder strap designs. Often, the entire skin of the gator was used, even the head and the claws. Domestic-made alligator bags were common as well as those made in Cuba and South America, particularly Brazil. In 1953, Sears sold alligator bags with or without the head and the claws for the price of $16.98, for either style. Two years earlier, the Lee-Robert Company offered genuine domestic alligator bags, which were leather lined, retailing for $49.50 to $85.00 each. Lizard and snakeskin handbags were also fashionable. Genuine snakeskin handbags were offered from Spiegel retailing for $7.98 each, while simulated snakeskin bags were considerable less at $2.98.

The filigree jewel box bag was another favorite in the fifties. The body of the bag was a gold-colored metal filigree and the top and handle were made of acetate and rayon faille. The inside of the bag contained a full mirror and a rayon lining. This particular bag was available in navy blue, black or brown and it sold for $3.59. Rayon velvet pouch bags were quite common either studded with rhinestones or sequins and especially favored for evening wear. They retailed for about $5.00 each.

In 1955, manufactured wicker basket bags were in vogue decorated with artificial fruit and flowers and styled for spring and summer wear. Palm leave basket bags, imported from Spain, were also stylish. Other summer varieties were drawstring pouches made of Chinese straw. They sold for $1.98. Fitted clutch bags made of fabric or leather were popular in addition to "Mother and Daughter" bags made of woven nylon. Barrel-shaped bags, boxy handbags, fitted vanity bags, shoulder bags, wing pouches, cushion pouches, satchels, panier handle and deep-shirred drawstring bags were the height of fashion. The styles were endless.

Patchwork underarm bag made of imitation lizard skin with Prystal zipper pull.

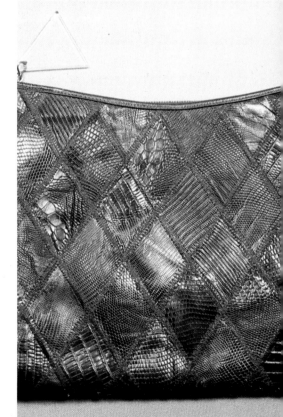

BEAUTIFULLY STYLED ALLIGATOR HANDBAGS

Alligator handbags offered for sale in 1966.

$85.00 was the retail price for this genuine alligator handbag featured in the Lee-Robert Company catalogue in 1951.

The Filigree Jewel Box Bag, Sears, 1953.

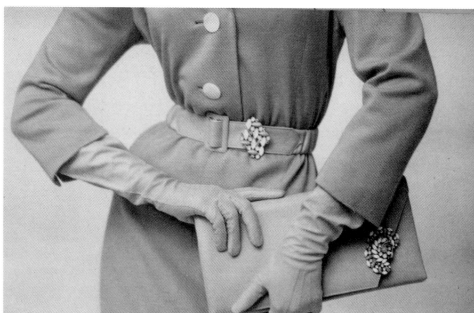

Envelope underarm bag decorated with jeweled clasp and matching jeweled ornament on belt, circa 1958.

$3.59
Tax Included

The Filigree Jewel Box-Bag

Pretty as a jewel box, luscious acetate and rayon faille smiles through fabulous gold-color metal filigree. Full-view mirror to see your pretty face inside top. Rayon lining. About 7¾x4 inches. Shipping weight 1 pound 6 ounces.
88 D 559E—Black............$3.59
88 D 560E—Dark brown....... 3.59
88 D 561E—Navy blue....... 3.59

Cobra handbag, dyed green, marked "Bags by Sterling, Genuine Reptile."

New machine made tapestry bag.

Large alligator bag, leather lined with two inside compartments and zippered pocket, marked "Genuine Alligator Made in Cuba."

Circa 1958.

Tapestry handbag with plastic frame, marked Bobbie Jerome.

By the late fifties and into the early sixties, handmade needlepoint bags enjoyed a revival. Needlecraft publications offered kits for creating wonderful needlepoint bags at home for fractions of the cost of the imported bags. The usual method of construction was to work the entire canvas, finishing the central design and the background. With the kits that were offered at this time, however, the central design was already completed and one had only to fill the background. After that task was completed it was attached to a finished lining and frame. These needlepoint kits ranged in price from $6.99 to $25.00 depending on the size of the bag and the complexity of the design.

The purse has gone through a long evolution throughout the centuries from the appended bags and pouches of embroidered cloth and leather that were used by both men and women, to the revolutionary lucite purses that created a fashion statement in the middle of the twentieth century. Although the terms pocketbook, purse and handbag have been used synonymously throughout the ages, their basic purpose has remained constant.

See additional advertisements for handbags of the nineteen fifties on page 182.

Clear lucite handbag enriched with thin layer of pearlized plastic, unmarked.

Crocheted gimp reticule accented with imitation pearls and metallic thread.

Rich-colored floral fabric makes this top handled bag very lovely. The inside is lined with grosgrain and marked Margaret Smith, Gardiner, Maine.

Lucite handbag with satin lining, slide closure and mesh strap handle, marked Evans.

Metal basket weave bag with plastic top marked Majestic.

Dyed green calf bag accented with goldtone metal straps forming squares. The inside of the bag is lined with grosgrain, marked ETRA.

2761 · *Medallion* · *About $12.00

2764 · *Victorian Rose* · *About $15.00
Petitpoint Center

2762 · *Medals* · *About $24.00
Crown Reverse Side

2763 · *Crown* · *About $17.00
Medals Reverse Side

Four different designs for making needlepoint handbags in 1961.

Barrel-shaped calfskin bag with double strap handles.

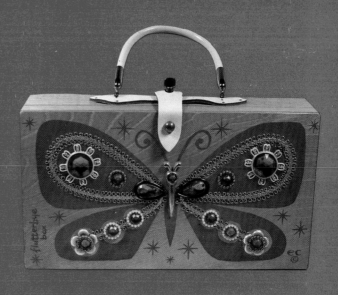

Wooden box-style bag with leather trim hand-decorated with beads, glass stones, gold braid and painted butterfly. The inside of the bag contains a large mirror and the bag is marked "The Original Box Bag by Collins of Texas, hand-decorated for you!" Copyright 1966 by Enid Collins.

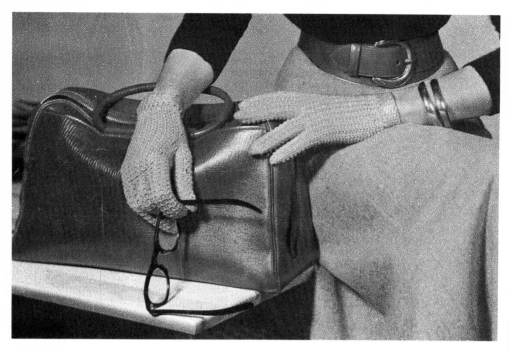

Calfskin bag and belt set by Greatrex,
circa 1953.

Wooden purse and matching notebook
made in Italy.

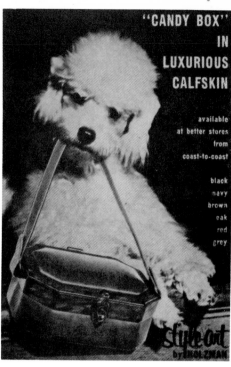

The "Candy Box" handbag made of
calfskin by Holzman, circa 1953.

Handbag decorated with silk-screened
floral design.

❧ Handbags in Advertising

Women's Leather Hand Bags, All Ready Sellers

LB. 2853. Seal grain and fancy embossed bag, cloth lining, 9-inch fancy ornamented frame, push lock, strap handle. Size 10½x7¼ inches.
Dozen $2.00

LB. 4092. Velvet hand bag, glass fringe on bottom, fancy cloth lining, 7 inch French gray finish frame, cord handle. Size 7½x6½ inches.
Dozen $4.00
LB. 4093. Same as above, smaller.
Dozen $2.00
LB. 4127. Velvet hand bag, poplin lining, 7-inch French grey finish frame, decorated, fringe on bottom of bag, cord handle. Size 7x6 inches.
Dozen $4.25
LB. 4106. Velvet hand bag, moire lining, 9-inch half oval French grey finish, fancy ornamented frame, silk cord handle. Size 9x7½ inches.
Dozen $4.25

LB. 2942. Velvet hand bag, moire lining, 9-inch French grey finish fancy ornamented frame, double strap handle. Size 8x10 inches.
Dozen $9.00

LB. 6430. Seal grain avenue bag, four pockets, extra flap on front, gilt button fastener and four gilt protected corners, 8-inch gilt finish frame, ball knobs, strap handle. Size 9x6½ inches.
Dozen $4.00

LB. 2962. Seal grain leather hand bag, gusseted ends, welted, tan imitation leather lining, extra pocket inside with purse, 9-inch fancy ornamented grey finish frame, double strap handle. Size 9x10½ inches.
Dozen $8.40

LB. 2949. Seal grain hand bag, gusseted ends, welted, black leather lining, reinforced gussets, extra pocket inside with purse, 8-inch half oval rose gold fancy ornamented frame, large knobs, double strap handle. Size 11x9 inches.
Each $1.25

LB. 4130. Seal grain hand bag, gusseted ends, welted, imitation leather lining, fitted with card case, purse, and mirror, 9-inch fancy ornamented mat silver finish frame, double strap handle. Size 10½x8 inches.
Dozen $4.00
LB. 2954. Seal grain hand bag, gusseted ends, welted, cloth lining, three pockets inside fitted with mirror, bottle and coin purse, 9-inch half oval French grey finish fancy ornamented frame, double strap handle. Size 10½x8¼ inches.
Dozen $4.25

LB. 8003. Newest imported lady's pocket book, size 4½x2¾ inches, made of sapphire leather, with nickel spring lock and frame, inside broken bottom, has the appearance of a dollar book.
Dozen $1.90

LB. 10|1720. Latest indestructible lady's pocket book, size 4x2¼ inches, made of fine morocco leather all through. Has three compartments and one extra compartment for Bills, nice nickel lock and patent frame inside, with embossed stamp marked indestructible. It's one of the newest designs, and makes an exceptional seller.
Dozen $4.00

LB. 2902. Seal grain hand bag, gusseted ends, welted, moire lining, 9-inch fancy front French grey finish frame, double strap handle. Size 10½x9½ inches.
Dozen $4.00

P. 734. Misses' velvet chain purses, assorted colors. Embossed oxidized effect front frame. This attractive number is a winner.
Dozen 75c
Gross $8.75

734

LB. 6415. Seal grain Boulevard bag, four pockets, extra flap on front, 8-inch gilt finish frame, ball knobs, double strap handle. Size 10x6½ inches. **Dozen $4.00**

P. 130. Misses' chatelaine bags, made of assorted fancy leather in several shades, with chain attached
Dozen 40c. **Gross $4.50**

P. 1208. Children's chatelaine bags, silver and gilt frames, double chain, assorted colors gilt shamrock set with stones.
Dozen 75c. **Gross $8.50**
P. 1556. Wrist hand bag, calf finished leather, assorted colors, canvas lined, fancy nickel 2 ball frame with chain.
Dozen 80c. **Gross $9.00**

Leather and velvet handbags and children's chatelaine bags offered for sale in 1900.

Square coin purse made of polished silver, gold or gunmetal attached to 50-inch chain, circa 1900.

High Grade Leather Novelty Purses

P. 946. Universal World's Famous Purse, size 3x3, dull black sheep, highly polished, brass, nickel plated, close fitting, riveted frame with frame button lock, muslin lined tray pocket.
Dozen $2.00

P. 1260. Assortment. Combination Coin and Bill Folds, calf finished sheep, assorted colors, turned in edges and skiver lining, gusseted-under flap with button lock, bill folds in black with large bill wing with flap and button lock, either compartment can be opened independent of the other, size closed ¾x3½ inches.
Dozen $4.20

P. 264. Size 3½x6 inches, long shape Purse, pig grain. 2 ball, overlapping, nickeled, rivetted frame. **Dozen $2.00**

P. 8347. Long shape kid Purse, assorted colors, 3 ball catch, overlapping, nickel plated polished, riveted frame, one short and one long pocket, size 3x5½ inches. **Dozen $1.75**
P. 831. As above, in cheaper quality. **Dozen $1.40**

P. 17. Money pouch, assorted kid, depth 5 nches, heavy leather tabs, two draw strings, extra inside pocket. **Dozen $1.75**

P. 8500. Continental Purse, dull black calf finished sheep, assorted colors, tray pocket with reinforced leather frame, extra leather pocket with flap and button lock, size 2¾x3 inches.
Dozen $4.00

P. 8545. Size 2x3½ inches, novelty purse, dull black calf, finished sheep, 2 ball catch, nickeled, polished, riveted, overlapping frame, pocket for sliding coin, leather top. **Dozen $1.75**

P. 195. Size 3½x5½ inches, long shape, kid Purse, three ball catch, nickeled, riveted frame, one short and one long pocket. **Dozen $1.50**
P. 831. As above, cheaper grade. **Dozen 85c.**

P. 192. Size 3x6 inches, long Purse, kid assorted colors, 2 ball catch, overlapping, highly polished, nickel plated, riveted frame. **Dozen $1.50**

P. 947. Universal Purse, black calf finished sheep, highly polished, brass, nickel plated, riveted frame, press button lock, tray style pocket for exposing coin, extra leather pocket with flap and button lock, size 3x3 inches.
Dozen $3.25

P. 8420. Size 2¼x4 inches, universal Purse, smooth, calf finished sheep, assorted colors, brass, highly polished, nickel plated, close fitting riveted frame, push button lock, muslin lined tray pocket, extra leather pocket, gusseted, with flap and button lock.
Dozen $4.20

P. 8406. Size 3x3½ inches, buck, highly polished, nickel plated brass, overlapping, frame side press button catches, spring opening, chamois lining, welted seams.
Dozen $2.25

P. 8540. Thin Model Universal Purse, calf finished sheep, assorted colors, size 3x3 inches, brass, nickel plated, highly polished, thin press frame with push button catch, riveted, regular coin pocket, one extra gusseted pocket with flap and button lock.
Dozen $3.60

P. 700. Assorted kid Purses, flat shape, 2 ball catch, brass, nickel plated, highly polished, riveted frame, By pulling knob (see cut) patent movable partition will open, exposing secret pocket, chamois lining, welted seams, size 3x3½ inches.
Dozen $4.00

P. 8346. Long shape farmer Purse, kid assorted colors, two ball catch, nickeled, riveted frame, **Dozen $1.50**
P. 829. As above, in cheaper goods. **Dozen 75c**

P. '648. Size, closed 2¾x2¾ inches, Quaker Purse, black calf, finished sheep leather lined, tray pocket for sliding coin into view, leather pocket with flap.
Dozen $2.00

P. 931. Assortment. Novelty Purse, highly polished, brass, riveted, 3 fold frame, with leather flap and button lock, box shaped pocket, 2 buttons, lined. **Dozen $2.00**
P. 955. As above, box shaped, coin pocket with three fold, secret bill pocket in back with snap button, coin pocket can be opened without displaying bill pocket, size closed 2¼x2½ inches.
Dozen $4.00

Leather novelty coin purses featured in the M. Gerber wholesale catalogue, circa 1900.

Leather trick purses featured in the M. Gerber catalogue, circa 1900.

Leather and Trick Purses

All Staple Numbers and Ready Sellers.

801 103 805 809 810

P. 801.	Black 2 ball purse, brown and tan kid leathers.	Dozen 18c.	Gross $2.00
P. 802.	Leather Purse, 2 ball snap and riveted frame, brown and black colors.	Dozen 23c.	Gross $2.50
P. 103.	Dongola Purse, medium size, in black and brown kid, assorted fancy riveted frames.	Dozen 28c.	Gross $3.00
P. 804.	3½x3 inches, nickel overlapping frame. black and brown leather.	Dozen 40c.	Gross $4.50
P. 805.	3 ball fancy nickel frame, genuine black leather, kid lined, size 3½x3 inches.	Dozen 70c.	
P. 809.	Size 3½x3 inches, fine black leather Purse, 2 pockets, leather lined.	Dozen 60c.	
P. 810.	Extra large Purse, with 4 ball frame, 4½x3½ inches.	Dozen 75c.	

P. 80. 2 ball, catch, nickel, riveted, frame, fancy edge, brown kid leather, size 3x3¾ inches.
Dozen 75c.

P. 819. Size 3x4½ inches, oblong shape, large Purse, made of fine stock, black leather lined, 3 ball top, nickel polished frame.
Dozen $1.20

P. 634. Assorted K id made of 1 piece of leather, seamless, block bottom, chamois lining, 3 ball catch, brass, nickel plated,, riveted frame, two pockets, size 3x3½ inches. **Dozen $1.50**

P. 8155. Size 2¾x3½ inches, gusseted bottom Purse, kid assorted colors, 2 ball catch, nickel plated polished frame, fancy etched design on sides and top, chamois lining, welted seams. **Dozen $1.75**

P. 8460. Kid Purse, flat shape, highly polished, nickel plated, overlapping frame, with patent turned catch lock, spring opening, chamois lining, welted seams, size 3½x3½ inches. **Dozen $2.00**

P. 249. Gusseted bottom Purse, kid assorted colors, size 3x3½ inches, 3 ball catch, nickel polished, riveted frame, two pockets, chamois lining, welted seams. **Dozen $1.90**

P. 229. Buck, Purse flat shape, 3 parts, nickel riveted frame, press button lock and centre partitions, 2 pockets, chamois lining, size 3¼x3½ inches.
Dozen 75c.

P. 8406. Buck Purse, flat shape, highly polished, nickel plated brass, overlapping frame side press button catches, spring opening, chamois lining, welted seams, size 3x3½ inches.
Dozen $1.25

P. 8032. Size 2½x3¾ inches bag shape purse, assorted smooth sheep, 2 ball catch, brass, highly polished, nickel plated, press frame, gusseted ends, welted seams, extra inside coin pocket, leather lining.
Dozen $2.00

P. 165. Size 3x3½ inches, imported combination trick purse, fine assorted leathers, nickel riveted frame with patent combination lock, fine chamois lining with instruction slips how to open.
Dozen $1.65

P. 994|7. Description same as P. 165, with the exception of the combination.
Dozen $1.65

P. 2647-7. Description same as P. 165, with the exception of the combination. **Dozen $1.65**

NOVELTY CHATELAINES ON PADS.

31257 Put up on fancy embossed lithographed printed cards in colors, size of card 5½x7, handsome chromo picture centers. Pad holds for display 1 dozen Chatelaines with fancy embossed pendants, suspended from which is a combination polished grooved pattern pearl in heart and ring shapes, with a swinging claw mounting, set with 2K size Kimberly natural color brilliants. Per Pad of 1 doz.   95

31258 Size of card 5½x7½, representing a handsome series of embossed and lithographed printed designs, with popular chromo portrait and scenic centers; pad holds for display 1 dozen assorted style Chatelaines, in plain and Roman gold finish, fancy embossed pins, suspended from which are a popular variety of heart, round and other pendants in fancy embossed and steel cut ornamentations, hard enamel inlaid, raised ornament, set with solitaire and groupings of oriental polished beads in all colors. Per pad of 1 dozen   95

31259 Size of card 7½x5½, tied with picot edge ribbon bows, card represents a popular series of embossed lithographed chromos in flower, portrait and scenic designs, fancy embossed pins, suspended from which is a representive line of pearl trimmed novelties, consisting of locks, harps, shoes, etc., the most reliable line of popular price chatelaines in the market. Per pad of 1 dozen   95

French Chatelaine.

31255 French Chatelaine, consisting of minia- doz. ture pattern watches, pendant from fleur de lis pin ornaments, embossed and enamel inlaid in all colors, put up on cards of 1

NOVELTY CHATELAINES ON PADS—Continued.

31260 The Vermicelli Locket, fine bright gold-plate patterns, star center, two glass covered picture spaces on inside, put up one dozen on display cards.... doz. 1 25

31262 Bird series of popular price Chatelaines, put up on a card. Each card in a carton, 6 cards to the box, all parts of bird or pendant ornaments are embossed and set with polished oriental beads in groupings of colors. (Illustration shows style of package.) **Doz.**   1 85

CHATELAINE ✦ THE LUCKY TRIO. ✦

31263 The Lucky Trio; accompanying illustra- doz. tion shows a display carton which holds 1 dozen of these popular chatelaines. The combination consists of a 4-leaf clover with brilliant steel cut ornamentation and hard enamel inlaying, plain silver finished horseshoe and a natural rabbit paw, with a crown pattern capping.   1 85

CHATELAINES.

32147 The very latest doz. and most popular selling chatelaine, in a hammered brass pattern, set consists of glove buttoner, pencil holder, celluloid writing tablet, set with one 4K size brilliant cut stone..1 75

CHATELAINES—Continued.

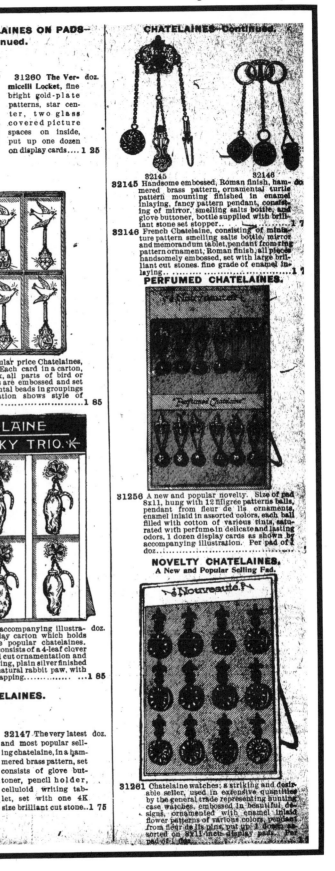

32145 **32146**

32145 Handsome embossed, Roman finish, ham- doz. mered brass pattern, ornamental turtle pattern mounting finished in enamel inlaying, fancy pattern pendant, consisting of mirror, smelling salts bottle, and glove buttoner, bottle supplied with brilliant stone set stopper..   17

32146 French Chatelaine, consisting of minia- ture pattern smelling salts bottle, mirror and memorandum tablet, pendant from ring pattern ornament, Roman finish, all pieces handsomely embossed, set with large brilliant cut stones. fine grade of enamel inlaying..   17

PERFUMED CHATELAINES.

31256 A new and popular novelty. Size of pad 8x11, hung with 12 filigree patterns balls, pendant from fleur de lis ornaments, enamel inlaid in assorted colors, each ball filled with cotton of various tints, saturated with perfume in delicate and lasting odors, 1 dozen display cards as shown by accompanying illustration. Per pad of 1 doz.

NOVELTY CHATELAINES.
A New and Popular Selling Fad.

31261 Chatelaine watches; a striking and desirable seller, used in extensive quantities by the general trade representing hunting case watches, embossed in beautiful designs, ornamented with enamel inlaid flower patterns of various colors, pendant from fleur de lis pins, put up 1 dozen assorted on 8x11 inch display pads. Per pad of 1

Novelty chatelaines offered for sale in 1899.

The Designer, January, 1905.

Circa 1918.

McCall's, September, 1910.

McCall's, June, 1911.

Circa 1911.

Circa 1911.

Circa 1910.

Circa 1912.

Circa 1912.

Circa 1912.

Knitting bag, circa 1917.

Circa 1918.

Circa 1918.

Crocheted bag and matching belt, circa
1918.

Mrs. Angier B. Duke carrying a draw-string reticule, *Harper's Bazaar*, December 1918.

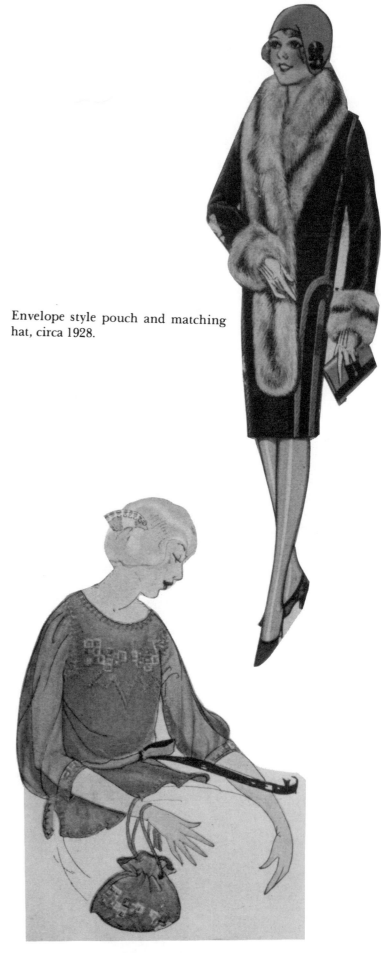

Envelope style pouch and matching hat, circa 1928.

Cross stitch (Slavic embroidery) drawstring reticule and matching blouse, circa 1922.

Simple BUT Very Smart!

Lane Bryant, circa 1929.

National Bellas Hess Company, circa 1928.

Lane Bryant, circa 1929.

These 1920s childrens' handbags were made almost identical to the adult models.

Genuine Leather Underarm Bag

Gift No. 2636 given free and postpaid for Six yearly subscriptions at 50 cents each

THIS type of pocketbook is very much in demand at present—and beside being fashionable, it is most serviceable. It is 8¼x4¼ inches when closed and made of an excellent grade of dark-brown cowhide. The lining is mercerized moire of a light-tan color; it has the usual inside compartments, one which closes with a metal clasp. One of the side pockets contains a mirror and small coin-purse. The front of the bag is tooled in a very pleasing design which shows in the illustration. This is done in dull tones of red and green and is the making of the bag. We chose this bag from among dozens of different numbers as the one which would give the most service and satisfaction to our readers. Truly it is a bargain at the small number of subscriptions asked. Order by name and number.

NEEDLECRAFT MAGAZINE
Augusta, Maine

Leather underarm bag, circa 1927.

Handbags of Smart Leather

$1.48

Ostrich, Calfskin, Reptile Grains!

Hundreds of new bags have just arrived to join this Anniversary price group. Black, blues, greens, tans, browns, novelties! Underarm, pouch, envelope, strap style.

Leather handbags offered for sale from Gimbel Bros. in October, 1929.

The New Bag With "Prystal" Frame

This is the much talked about bag of exquisitely fine antelope with the very new frame of prystal which is one of the sensations of bagdom.

And what is prystal? An ultra smart composition which looks like crystal in plain and frosted effect.

Beautifully made—note the smart little self-tab at the front. An adorable inside purse. **$14.95.**

A Black Antelope Bag, imported from France, wears a brilliant ornament of chrysoprase and marcasite.

$29.95

Black antelope bag advertised for sale in 1929.

Antelope bag with Prystal frame, circa 1929.

Beaded Bags

All the bags on this page are imported direct from Paris and are so labeled on the inside.

J861/61—Backgrounds of blue, grey, green or brown; assorted patterns, silk lined; size 7½x7 inches ....**Each 33.00**

J861/63—Backgrounds of grey or blue; patterns in various colors, silk lined; size 9x6¼ inches.. ....**Each 40.00**

J861/83—Backgrounds of blue or yellow assorted colored patterns, silk lined; size 7½x5½ inches....**Each 40.00**

J861/62—Combination patterns, in blue and gold or yellow and brown; silk taffeta lined; size 8x 6½ inches ....**Each 36.00**

J861/72—Backgrounds of blue or jet, pattern in silver, silk lined; shell frame; size 9x6½ inches.... ....**Each 50.00**

J861/87—All cut steel beads, croched oriental effects in bright colors; ribbon style handle: size 4¼x3 inches ....**Each 27.00**

J861/89—All fine steel cut beads; croched in beautiful patterns, no two alike; size 8x6½ inches...... ....**Each 90.00**

J861/75—Background of green; various colored patterns; ivory frame; silk lined: size 9½x8½ inches ....**Each 90.00**

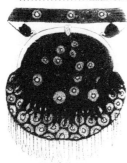   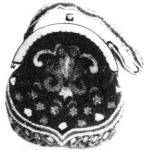

J861/74—A pretty combination of blue, red, green, gold and jet; ivory frame, silk lined; size 9¼x8¼ inches ......**Each 100.00**

J861/81—Background of blue, patterns in various colors, silk lined; shell and amber frames; size 8x8 inches......**Each 75.00**

J861/78—Background of blue; bright colored patterns, silk lined; shell and white ivory frames: size 9½x7½ inches ......**Each 75.00**

J861/66—Backgrounds of purple or brown; patterns in bright colors, silk lined; shell frame; size 8x7½ inches.....**Each 70.00**

J861/80—Background of yellow, various colored patterns, silk lined; amber frame; size 9½x7½ inches ....**Each 65.00**

J861/65—Backgrounds of blue or green, bright colored patterns, silk lined; two compartments; size 10¼x6¾ inches..**Each 36.00**

J861/77—Background of blue, patterns in gold, jet, red and white; silk lined; shell frame; size 10½x8 inches....**Each 85.00**

J861/68—Backgrounds of blue or red; patterns in bright colors; silk lined; fine frame: size 8½x 7¼ inches ....**Each 60.00**

French beaded bags offered for sale in 1920.

No. 56413. White Enamel Mesh, Zipper Top, Silver Plated Back Strap Handle. Moire Silk Lining. Size 8½x5½ Inches..........$6.00

No. 56414. 6-Inch Nickel Silver Plated Frame and Handle. Two-Tone Black and White Enamel Mesh. Moire Silk Lining............$4.50

No. 56415. Two-Tone Blue and White Enamel Mesh. Zipper Top. Silver Plated Back Strap Handle. Moire Silk Lining. Size 7x5½ Inches..........$4.50

No. 56416. 6-Inch Nickel Silver Plated Frame and Handle. White Enamel Mesh. Moire Silk Lining............$4.50

No. 56417. 6-Inch Nickel Silver Plated Frame and Handle. Two-Tone Brown and Buff Enamel Mesh. Moire Silk Lining..........$4.50

No. 56418. Two-Tone Black and White Enamel Mesh. Zipper Top. Silver Plated Back Strap Handle. Moire Silk Lining. Size 8½x5½ Inches............$6.00

No. 56419. 3-Inch Frame. Enamel Beadlite Mesh. Pearl Finish. Black Enamel Frame..........$3.75

No. 56420. 4-Inch Frame. Nickel Silver Plated. Two-Tone Black and White Enamel Tile Mesh............$1.25
No. 56421. Same, in All White Enamel............1.25

No. 56422. 3-Inch Frame. Dresden Enamel Mesh. Enamel Frame. Assorted Colors............$1.80

No. 56423. 3-Inch Frame. Silver Plate. Armor Mesh. Enameled Light and Dark Blue, Light and Dark Green, or Red and Yellow Color Combinations. Silver Plated Chain............$2.00

No. 56424. 3¼-Inch Dark Green Enamel Frame. Green Enameled Armor Mesh. Silver Plated Chain. Moire Silk Lined..........$2.50

No. 56425. 3-Inch Frame. Silver Plated. Armor Mesh. Enameled Black and White Combination. Silver Plated Chain. Each............$2.00

No. 56426. Coin Purse. 2-Inch Frame; Silver Plated. Fine Soldered Mesh. Silver Plated Chain..........$3.00

No. 56427. 4-Inch Nickel Silver Plated Frame. White Enamel Baguette Mesh. Nickel Silver Chain. Moire Silk Lined; with Mirror............$3.75

No. 56428. 3-Inch Frame. Silver Plate. Armor Mesh. Enameled Light and Dark Blue Color Combination. Silver Plated Chain............$2.00

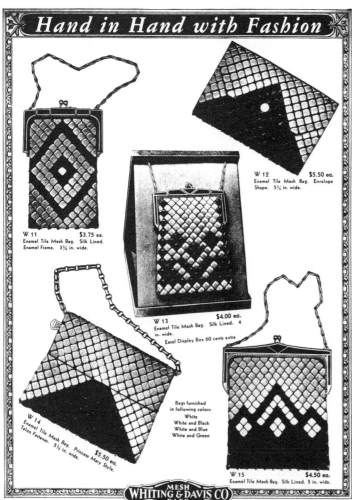

Hand in Hand with Fashion

W 11 $3.75 ea.
Enamel Tile Mesh Bag. Silk Lined. Enamel Frame. 3¾ in. wide.

W 12 $5.50 ea.
Enamel Tile Mesh Bag. Envelope Shape. 5¾ in. wide.

W 13 $4.00 ea.
Enamel Tile Mesh Bag. Silk Lined. 4 in. wide.
Easel Display Box 60 cents extra

W 14 $5.50 ea.
Enamel Tile Mesh Bag. Princess Mary Style. Talon Fastener. 5¾ in. wide.

Bags furnished in following colors:
White
White and Black
White and Blue
White and Green

W 15 $4.50 ea.
Enamel Tile Mesh Bag. Silk Lined. 5 in. wide.

WHITING & DAVIS CO
MESH BAGS
TRADE MARK REG. U.S. AND CAN.

227

No. 56405. 5-Inch Gold Plate. English Finish Frame, Chain and Armor Mesh. Silk Lining with Mirror............$5.50

No. 56406. 5-Inch Nickel Silver Plated Frame and Chain. Black Enamel Shell Effect Mesh. Silk Lining with Mirror............$5.00
No. 56407. Same in White............5.00

No. 56408. Enamel "Beadlite" Mesh Bag. Pearl Finish. Silk Lining. with Mirror. Zipper Top with Draw Chain. Size 6½ x 4½ Inches. Very Light Weight......$3.75

No. 56409. Silver Plate Baguette Mesh. Silk Lining with Mirror. Zipper Top with Draw Chain. Size 6½ x 4½ Inches. Very Light Weight............$3.50

No. 56410. Chromium Plated Mesh. Nickel Silver Plated Draw Chain and Rings. Moire Silk Lining. Size 6 x 4½ Inches............$3.00

No. 56411. Navy Blue Enamel Mesh. Silver Plated Draw Chain and Rings. Moire Silk Lining. Size 6 x 4½ Inches............$3.30

No. 56412. Chromium Plated Mesh. Nickel Silver Plated Draw Chain and Rings. Moire Silk Lining. Size 6 x 4 Inches............$3.00

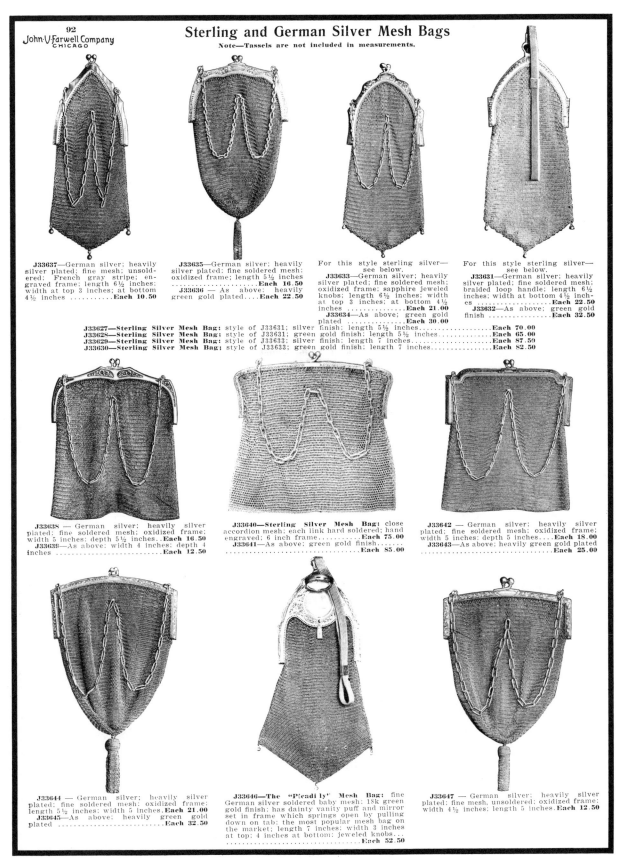

92
John·V·Farwell Company
CHICAGO

Sterling and German Silver Mesh Bags
Note—Tassels are not included in measurements.

J33637—German silver; heavily silver plated; fine mesh; unsoldered; French gray stripe; engraved frame; length 6½ inches; width at top 3 inches; at bottom 4½ inches ....**Each 10.50**

J33635—German silver; heavily silver plated; fine soldered mesh; oxidized frame; length 5½ inches ....**Each 16.50**
J33636 — As above; heavily green gold plated....**Each 22.50**

For this style sterling silver— see below.
J33633—German silver; heavily silver plated; fine soldered mesh; oxidized frame; sapphire jeweled knobs; length 6½ inches; width at top 3 inches; at bottom 4½ inches ....**Each 21.00**
J33634—As above; green gold plated ....**Each 30.00**

For this style sterling silver— see below.
J33631—German silver; heavily silver plated; fine soldered mesh; braided loop handle; length 6½ inches; width at bottom 4½ inches ....**Each 22.50**
J33632—As above; green gold finish ....**Each 32.50**

J33627—**Sterling Silver Mesh Bag**; style of J33631; silver finish; length 5½ inches...................**Each 70.00**
J33628—**Sterling Silver Mesh Bag**; style of J33631; green gold finish; length 5½ inches............**Each 65.00**
J33629—**Sterling Silver Mesh Bag**; style of J33633; silver finish; length 7 inches.................**Each 87.50**
J33630—**Sterling Silver Mesh Bag**; style of J33633; green gold finish; length 7 inches................**Each 82.50**

J33638 — German silver; heavily silver plated; fine soldered mesh; oxidized frame; width 5 inches; depth 5½ inches. **Each 16.50**
J33639—As above; width 4 inches; depth 4 inches ....**Each 12.50**

J33640—**Sterling Silver Mesh Bag**; close accordion mesh; each link hard soldered; hand engraved; 6 inch frame...........**Each 75.00**
J33641—As above; green gold finish.......**Each 85.00**

J33642 — German silver; heavily silver plated; fine soldered mesh; oxidized frame; width 5 inches; depth 5 inches....**Each 18.00**
J33643—As above; heavily green gold plated ....**Each 25.00**

J33644 — German silver; heavily silver plated; fine soldered mesh; oxidized frame; length 5½ inches; width 5 inches. **Each 21.00**
J33645—As above; heavily green gold plated ....**Each 32.50**

J33646—The "Picadily" Mesh Bag; fine German silver soldered baby mesh; 18k green gold finish; has dainty vanity puff and mirror set in frame which springs open by pulling down on tab; the most popular mesh bag on the market; length 7 inches; width 3 inches at top; 4 inches at bottom; jeweled knobs... ....**Each 52.50**

J33647 — German silver; heavily silver plated; fine mesh, unsoldered; oxidized frame; width 4½ inches; length 5 inches.**Each 12.50**

Opposite page:
Mesh bags advertised by Benjamin Allen & Co., Inc., circa 1935.

Baby fine mesh bags featured in the John V. Farwell Company catalogue of 1920.

Mesh Bags and Bag Tops

John·V·Farwell Company
CHICAGO

J33648—Mesh Bag: German silver; heavily silver plated; fine mesh; unsoldered; oxidized frame; width 4 inches; depth 5 inches......
.............................**Each 8.00**
J33649—Mesh Bag: German silver; heavily silver plated; fine mesh; unsoldered; oxidized frame; width 4 inches; depth 4 inches.......
.............................**Each 7.25**

J33650—Mesh Bag: German silver; heavily silver plated; fine mesh, unsoldered; oxidized frame; width 5½ inches; depth 5 inches.....
.............................**Each 10.50**

J33651—Mesh Bag: German silver; heavily silver plated; oxidized frame; unsoldered mesh; width 4½ inches; depth 4 inches.....
.............................**Each 7.50**

J33652—Bag Top: silver plated; French gray finish; assorted patterns; size 6 inches.
.............................**Each 75c**

Showing silk bag made from frame similar to those shown above.

J33653—Bag Top: width 6 inches; oxidized silver plated; applied ornaments; colored jewel settings ....**Each 1.25**
J33654—As above; more jewels..**Each 1.50**

J33655—Bag Top: silver plated; oxidized; size 6 inches.....................**Each 2.00**

J33656—Bag Top: silver plated: French gray finish; size 6 inches.........**Each 1.50**
J33657—As above; jeweled......**Each 1.75**

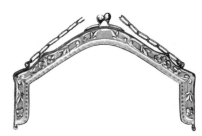

J33658—Bag Top: extra quality; silver plated; French gray finish; size 6 inches........
.............................**Each 4.00**

J33659—Bag Top: silver plated; oxidized finish; especially fine for a velvet bag; size 7 inches ....**Each 4.50**

J33660—Bag Top: extra quality silver plated; French gray finish; size 6½ inches......
.............................**Each 4.50**

J33661—Bag Top: silver plated; oxidized finish; size 6 inches...................**Each 1.50**

J33662—Bag Top: celluloid; shell effect; heavy stock; size 6 inches.........**Each 1.50**
J33663—As above; shaded blue and green..
.............................**Each 1.50**

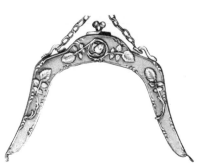

J33664—Bag Top: extra quality silver plated; French gray finish; rose design; size 6½ inches ....**Each 3.50**

John V. Farwell, circa 1920.

183

America's Most Exquisite Sterling Silver, Gold Plate and Silver Finish Mesh Bags

Only in the Exclusive Circle, Where Fashions Degree Predominates, Will You Find These Magnificent Bags in Vogue. Artistically Made and Beautifully Finished, Finest Durable Mesh Made. Every Link Soldered, Without Seams.

Milady's Most Perfect Gift

Come fitted with blue sapphire stone set clasp.

No. 7221　Silver finish; 3-inch frame; extreme length, including tassel, 8¼ inches, each.......................$59.50

No. 7222　Sterling silver; 3-inch frame; length, 6½ inches, each.............$86.50

Come fitted with blue sapphire stone set clasp.

No. 7223　Silver finish; 3¼-inch frame; extreme length, including tassel, 8¼ inches, each.......................$59.50

No. 7224　Gold plate, green gold Finish; 3¼-inch frame; extreme length, including tassel, 8¼ inches. Each.................$59.50

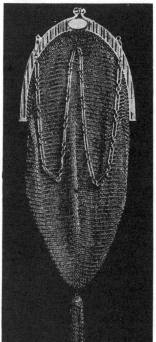

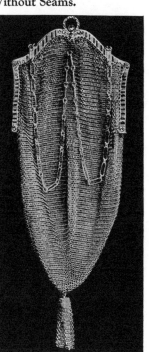

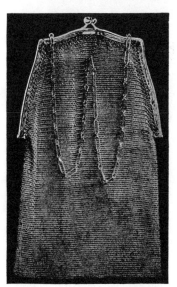

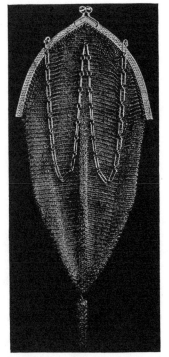

Come fitted with blue sapphire stone set clasp.

No. 7226　Silver finish; 3¼-inch frame; length, 6½ inches, each.............$53.00

No. 7227　Sterling silver; 3-inch frame; length, 5¾ inches, each.............76.50

No. 7228　Gold plate, green gold finish; 3¼-inch frame; length, 6½ inches, each. 53.00

Come fitted with blue sapphire stone set clasp.
No. 7225　Silver finish; 3½-inch frame; extreme length, including tassel, 8 inches, each.......................$59.50

Come fitted with blue sapphire stone set clasp.

No. 7229　Silver finish; 3¾-inch frame; length, 6 inches, each...............$56.50

Baby fine mesh bags offered for sale in 1923 from the Ft. Dearborn Watch and Clock Company.

3347

Butler Brothers Wholesale catalogue,
circa 1937.

McCall's August,
1939.

Talon Fastener advertisement, circa 1937.

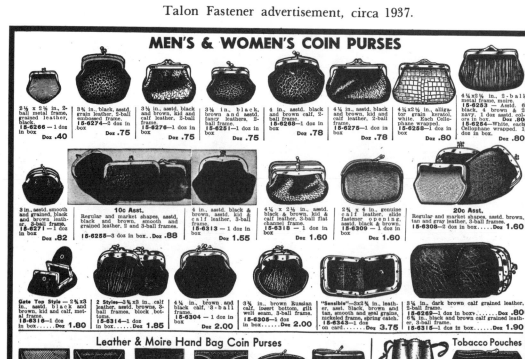

No. 1717. Bag Stamped on Canvas Including Colored Wools for Flower Motifs (12 shades). Price, $1.25. The only wool not given is the background wool. This may be in navy, gray, taupe or black. To make bag, 10 x 12 inches; or pillow 11 inches, or footstool. Full directions.

No. 1755. Suede Leather Bag with Monogram Applique. Price, $1.00. A fine quality of suede leather is given in any of the color combinations shown. A piece for coin purse also included, and matching beads for finishing edges and monogram. Size of bag 3¾ x 6¾ inches. Beading directions included.

No. 1636. Beauvais Bag Design Stamped on Black Silk Poplin. Price, $1.00. They are all the fashion, and if you work one yourself, not so very expensive. The black silk for front and back is provided ready stamped. You require the colored strand cottons for the simple chainstitch work, and bag top. Complete directions given for embroidering and finishing bag, size, 5¾ x 8 inches.

No. 1650. Envelope Bag Design Stamped on Canvas. Price, 45 cents. A small sized modernistic colored bag like this is the smartest thing to carry with your sports or street frock. To work it you use crepe twist double, in the long slanting stitches for leaves and flowers, and straight even stitches for the background. Full directions for making included, 3¾ x 7 inches.

No. 1599. Envelope Bag Design Stamped on Canvas. Price, 50 cents. You may work it in wools as shown in the blue illustration, with corners done in petit point stitch; or you may work it in crepe twist, and fill the flower centers with beads. Wool and crepe twist combined give an extremely smart effect also. Full directions given for working the bag, size 4¾ x 9¾ inches.

No. 1645. Bag Design for Italian Quilting (Blue) with Thin Lining Material Included. Price, 40 cents. Stamp the transfer for front and back of bag on the thin lining given in pattern, then baste them to your silk material for outside of bag, and quilt from the back as directed for Italian quilting. Size 8¼ x 12 inches, to be finished with a 9-inch frame top.

Wonderful transfer designs for bag making, McCall's Pattern Book, circa 1931.

Bags by Josef, *Vogue* September, 1947.

Large corde' underarm bag with Prystal zipper pull, circa 1940.

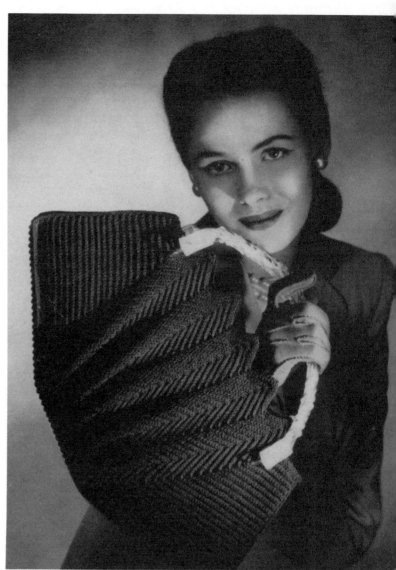

Corde' bag with Prystal handles, circa 1940.

McCall's March, 1943.

PATENT-LIKE PLASTICS are style news

they shine brightly as a Fall fashion

A $3.49
Tax included

B $8.88
Tax included

C $2.34
Tax included

D $5.89
Tax included

E $3.49
Tax included

F $6.99
Tax included

A DRESSMAKER FOLDS lend a soft touch to this inky black, patent-like plastic zip-top. Practical as well as pretty— won't peel or crack. Fabric lined, mirror. *Size* about 13¾ x 6¾ inches. Shpg. wt. 12 oz. 88 G 1903E—Black......3.49

B BUCKLE-FRONT, elegant in black patent-like plastic that won't peel. Front draped zip-top, shell-like ornament. Fabric lined, change purse, comb, mirror. *Size* about 15¼ x 8¾ in. Shipping weight 1 lb. 88 G 1902E—Black......8.88

C WEDGE SHAPE, neatly designed zip-top of bright black patent-like plastic, proof against peeling. Clever seams in front, mock shell pull. Fabric lined, mirror. *Size* abt. 10¾ x 6½ in. Shpg. wt. 10 oz. 88 G 1905E—Black......2.34

D MOCK SHELL FRAME, snaps open or shut without a lock, broad base for roominess. Mirror-bright black patent-like plastic that won't peel. Fabric lined, mirror. *Size* about 11 x 6½ in. Shipping weight 15 oz. 88 G 1901E—Black......5.89

E LOOP HANDLES, streamlined practical zip-top. Coal-black crackproof patent-like plastic. Lots of style news in the triangular detailing. Fabric lined, mirror. *Size* about 7½ x 8½ in. Shpg. wt. 12 oz. 88 G 1906E—Black......3.49

F QUILTED CUFF, a new trimming trend sets off the sleek black patent-like plastic of this roomy zip-top. Durable, won't crack. Fabric lined, coin case, mirror. *Size* about 17½ x 9 in. Shipping weight 1 pound. 88 G 1900E—Black......6.99

Prices of all bags illustrated include 20% Federal Excise Tax. Bags can be paid for on Easy Terms . . see inside back cover.

186 SEARS, ROEBUCK AND CO.

Patent-like plastic leather handbags
featured in the 1946 Sears catalogue.

Spring and Summer bags featured in
the Aldens catalogue of 1959.

❦ Bibliography

Books

Buck, Anne. *Victorian Costume and Costume Accessories.* New York: Thomas Nelson & Sons, 1961.

Caulfeild, S.F.A. *Encyclopedia of Victorian Needlework.* New York: Dover Publications, Inc., 1972.

Clabburn, Pamela. *Beadwork.* Great Britian: Shire Publications Ltd., 1989.

Clifford, Anne. *Cut Steel and Berlin Iron Jewellery.* Cranbury, New Jersey: A.S. Barnes & Co. Inc., 1971.

Cunnington, C. Willett and Phillis Cunnington. *Handbook of English Costume in the Nineteenth Century.* Great Britian: Dufour Editions, 1959.

Earle, Alice Morse. *Two Centuries of Costume in America.* New York: The Macmillan Company, 1903.

————— , *Costume of Colonial Times.* New York: Empire State Book Co., 1924.

Edwards, Joan. *Bead Embroidery.* New York: Taplinger Publishing Co., 1967.

Ewing, Elizabeth. *History of Twentieth Century Fashion.* London: BT Batsford Ltd., 1974.

Foster, Vanda. *Bags and Purses.* London: BT Batsford Ltd., 1982.

Gottlieb, Robert and Frank Maresca. *A Certain Style, The Art of the Plastic Handbag.* New York: Alfred A. Knopf, Inc., 1988.

Haertig, Evelyn. *Antique Combs and Purses.* Carmel, California: Gallery Graphics Press, 1983.

————— , *More Beautiful Purses.* Carmel, California: Gallery Graphics Press, 1990.

Holiner, Richard. *Antique Purses, A History, Identification and Value Guide.* Paducah, Kentucky: Collector Books, 1987.

Lester, Katherine M. *Accessories of Dress.* Peoria, Illinois: Chas. A. Bennett Co. Inc., 1954.

McClellan, Elisabeth. *Historic Dress in America.* New York: Benjamin Blom Inc., 1969.

Payne, Blanche. *History of Costume From Ancient Egypt to the Twentieth Century.* New York: Harper & Row Publishers, 1965.

Proctor, Molly G. *Victorian Canvas Work (Berlin Wool Work).* New York: Drake, 1972.

Schuette, Marie and Sigrid Muller-Christensen. *A Pictorial History of Embroidery.* New York: Frederick A. Praeger, 1964.

Seyd, Mary. *Introducing Beads.* London: BT Batsford, 1973.

Waterer, John W. *Spanish Leather.* London: Faber & Faber Ltd., 1971.

White, Mary. *How To Do Beadwork.* New York: Dover Publications, 1972.

Catalogs

Aldens, Chicago, Illinois, Spring and Summer, 1959.

Au Printemps, Paris, Fall, 1927.

Benj. Allen & Co. Inc., Chicago, Illinois, 1935.

Bennett Blue Book, Chicago and New York, 1966.

BHA Illustrated Catalogue, Schwenksville, Pennsylvania, 1895.

Bloomingdale's Illustrated 1886 Catalog, Dover Reprint, 1988.

Boston Store, Chicago, Illinois, Fall and Winter, 1910/1911.

Butler Brothers Dry Goods, January, 1937.

Carson Pirie Scott & Co., Chicago, Illinois, 1942.

Charles William Stores, New York, 1920 and 1925.

Chicago Mail Order Company, Chicago, 1911/1912.

Christie's East Auction Catalogs, New York, 1987 & 1988.

Fort Dearborn Watch & Clock Company, Chicago, 1923/1924.

Frederick Herrschner Inc., 1932/1933.

H.M.Manheim & Company, Catalogue #72, New York, 1933.

Holsman & Alter Company, Chicago, Illinois, 1898.

Jason Weiler & Sons, Boston, Mass., 1927.

John V. Farwell Company. Chicago, 1920/1921.

John Wanamaker Store & Home Catalogue, Philadelphia, 1913.

Joseph Hagn Company Wholesale Catalog, 1934/1935 and 1959.

Lane Bryant, New York, Spring and Summer, 1929.

Lee-Robert Company, Chicago, 1950/1951.

Lyon Brothers Catalog #258, Chicago, 1899-1900.
M. Gerber Wholesale Company, Philadelphia, 1899/1900.
Montgomery Ward & Company, Chicago, 1895, 1922, 1937/1938 and 1953.
National Bellas Hess Company, New York & Kansas City, 1928.
National Cloak & Suit Company, 1925.
Sears, Roebuck & Company, Chicago and Philadelphia, 1900, 1902, 1909, 1927, 1930, 1937, 1938, 1939, 1942, 1943-44, 1946-47, 1949, 1951, 1953, 1955 and 1963.
Sotheby's Auction Catalogs (Jewelry), New York, 1988, 1989, 1990 and 1991.
Spiegel, Spring and Summer, 1948 and 1951.

Magazines
Delineator (1884, 1902, 1928, 1932, 1933, and 1935).
Designer (1905, 1912 and 1923).
Ehrichs' Fashion Quarterly (1879, 1880 and 1882).
Godey's Lady's Book (1862).
Harper's Bazaar (1899, 1918, 1936, 1937, 1938, 1939, 1940 and 1957).
Home Arts Needlecraft (1930, 1932, 1934, 1938 and 1939).
Home Needlework Magazine (1903 and 1905).
Keystone (1919, 1920, 1922 and 1929).
Ladies' Home Journal (1891, 1893, 1897, 1903, 1909, 1912, 1928, 1933, 1944 and 1952).
Ladies' World (1906).
Life (1940, 1947, 1948, 1949, 1951 and 1953).
McCall's (1908, 1910, 1911, 1912, 1916, 1917, 1932, 1936, 1938, 1939, 1943 and 1949).
Modern Pricilla (March, 1916).
Needlecraft Magazine (1913, 1923, 1927, 1930, 1932 and 1934).
New York Times Magazine (March 1, 1953).
Peoples' Home Journal (November 1911).
Pictorial Review (1922, 1935 and 1936).
Ridley's Fashion Magazine (1882 and 1883).
Seventeen (1947, 1948 and 1958).
Today's Housewife (May 1923).
To-Day's Magazine (1911 and 1912).
Vogue (1917, 1918, 1919, 1936, 1937, 1938, 1939, 1947 and 1960).
Weldon's Ladies' Journal (October 1924).
Woman's Home Companion (1953 and 1955).
Woman's World (1919, 1922 and 1926).

Pattern Books
Bags & Hats, Fraser Manufacturing Co., New York.
Book of Filet Crochet & Cross Stitch, Book #7, Published by Cora Kirchmaier, 1920.
Bucilla Blue Book of Crochet, No. 11, 1917.
Crochet Design, No.12, M.Heminway & Sons, Watertown, Conn., 1917.
Crochet Design, War-time Economies in Crochet, H.K.H. Silk Co., 1918.
McCall's Complete Needlework, 1931, 1943, 1949, 1950, 1953 and 1961/1962.
Peter Pan Hat & Bag Book, Wool Trading Co., New York.
Royal Society Crochet Book, No.10, 1917.
Silk Purses & Bags and How To Make Them, Published by The Corticelli Silk Mills, Florence, Mass.

Newspapers
Evening Public Ledger, Philadelphia, June, October and December 1929 and 1930.
Happy Hours, 1913.
Philadelphia Inquirer, Philadelphia, June, October and December 1929 and 1930.

Values vary immensely according to an article's condition, location of the market, parts of the country, and overall quality of design. While one must make their own decisions, we can offer a guide. Handbags in original advertisements have not been valued.

SS- Sterling Silver   GS- German Silver   GF- Gold-filled

Chapter I

		US $
p-7.	Tapestry bag	300-400
p-11.	French Knot bag	100-150
p-12.	Ivory coin purse	200-300
p-14.	Petit Point bag	400-500
p-15.	Misers bags	50-100
p-16.	Metal purses	75-125
p-17.	Colonial purse	50-100
	Leather purse	40-50
p-18.	Gorham purse	300-350
p-23.	Shell purses	50-125
p-24.	Sovereign purses	50-95
p-25.	SS Finger ring purse	125-175

Chapter II

p-26.	SS Chatelaine	500-750
p-27.	GS Chatelaine bag	125-175
p-28.	Velvet chatelaine bag	250-350
p-29.	Beaded chatelaine bag	100-135
	Chat. coin holder	115-155
p-30.	Fr.Jet chatelaine bag	100-125
p-31.	Cut steel chat. bag	125-175
p-32	SS Finger ring purse	150-200
p-33.	GS Finger ring purse	90-125
	Mesh chatelaine bag	150-200
p-34.	Crocheted chat. bags	100-150

Chapter III

p-37.	Silk evening bag	50-100
	Antelope bag	100-140

p-38.	Rhinestone bag	60-80
	Celluloid bag	125-185
p-39.	Velvet bag	75-100
p-40.	Gold Kid bag	100-150
	Back strap pouch	65-95
p-42.	Pleated handbags	45-65
p-43.	Crocheted reticule	40-60
p-44.	Petit Point bags	275-400
	Needlepoint bags	100-150
p-45.	Needlepoint bags	125-225
p-46.	Tapestry bag	115-165
p-47.	Tapestry bag	75-125
p-50.	Metallic gauze bag	65-95
p-51.	Alligator bags	125-225
p-52.	Cartier bag	200-350
p-53.	Suede pouch	65-95
p-54-55.	Hand-tooled bags	50-250
p-58.	Tam O' Shanter	50-100

Chapter IV

p-61-63.	Beaded reticules	100-300
p-64-65.	Shaggy bead bags	140-225
p-66.	Shaggy bead reticule	100-125
	Beaded wrist bags	100-150
p-67.	Bag w/ plastic frame	110-165
p-69.	Bag w/ metal frame	175-225
p-70-71.	Cut steel bags	125-300
p-70.	Colored cut steel	300-450
p-72.	Cut steel bags	85-135
p-74.	Large beaded bag	175-225
p-75.	Bead network bag	135-160
	Czech. beaded bags	35-65
p-77-79.	Beaded box bags	75-150
p-80.	Large beaded ret.	200-350

✢ Index